LEADERSHIP

LEADERSHIP
Combat Leaders *and* Lessons

EDITORS

Colonel James L. Abrahamson, USA (Ret.)

and

Colonel Andrew P. O'Meara, Jr., USA (Ret.)

United States
Military Academy

Class of 1959

ISBN # 978-0-615-25574-3

Published by Stand Up America, USA

Bigfork, Montana

Printed in the United States of America

Dedicated to those who went into harm's way in the service of our country, protecting the precious legacy of freedom paid for by the sacrifices of generations of soldiers and leaders who defended the bright vision of our Founding Fathers.

TABLE *of* CONTENTS

PREFACE

Those called to the military profession draw inspiration from a rich heritage – a heritage bequeathed to them by individuals of courage and integrity who have protected our country throughout its history. In like manner the heritage of West Point draws cadets and graduates to the metaphor of the "Long Gray Line." Something in those formative early years, annealed by the life experiences of our distinctive calling, binds us in spirit, one to another. It is a remarkable, and durable, bond that extends from one generation to the next – tying lives from the past to those of the future. It exerts a powerful influence within the halls of West Point as well as throughout the larger community of those attracted to the military profession and making up our armed forces. Indeed, the reflections in this book are intended for all who seek enlightened leadership – throughout the entire American military, and beyond.

A soldier's profession is one of action. While all of life is a voyage into the unknown, the warrior's journey seems, somehow, unusually so. Much of what matters most comes not from abstract musing, but from the raw reality of the battlefield. It is the accumulated wisdom of informed, honest perspectives – "Lessons Learned" if you will – that lights the way to a less precarious, and hopefully more successful, path ahead.

That is the essence of this book. Prompted by an appeal from our West Point "affiliation" Class – that is, the one fifty years our "junior" – we set out to assemble a selected collection of our experiences. Twenty-five of them are included here. They focus on how, during the era of our active military careers, history and fate exposed our generation to the core realities of the Profession of Arms. Direct, forthright, honest, and frank, they do not seek to advance predisposed propositions, sugarcoat awkward truths, or deny weakness and shortcoming. They deal in facts, details and specifics. They chronicle, interpret and, I believe, teach. Neither self-righteous nor self-serving, they stand as expressions of how these particular leaders of character sought to live up to the ideal that General Douglas MacArthur described as "those three hallowed words"… Duty – Honor – Country.

How, you might ask, does a project like this come to be? The answer is through initiative, energy and a strong sense of purpose. In this instance, it must also be credited to the commitment and skill of two remarkable professionals, who willingly undertook the task of pulling it all together. Two graduates of the West Point Class of 1959 were especially qualified for the undertaking: Colonel Andy O'Meara and Colonel Jim Abrahamson. They are two quite different people, whose careers followed very different paths. Yet, together, they bring an amalgam of views that contributes powerfully to the balance and insight of this book.

Andy is the consummate warrior. He possesses a perspective that reflects extensive service with troops and personal combat experience, including two tours in Vietnam, where he was seriously wounded and earned the Silver Star for bravery. He holds a visceral sense of the poignancy of life and death on the battlefield and a profound respect for the uncommon dignity of the individual soldier. Jim, on the other hand, is not only a soldier, with Vietnam service, like Andy, in the 11th Armored Cavalry Regiment but – by dint of training and decades of teaching as a college professor – a professional historian, as well. As a life-long student of the art and science of warfare, he contributes to this work a thoughtful sense of time, tint, and context.

Whatever the talents of the editors, they could assemble this book only because members of the Class took time to reflect on the lessons they had learned, and then plumbed their private and innermost reflections to offer perspectives they thought might be instructive and useful. Though limitations of space meant that not all their submissions found a place in the book's final form, the Class owes a debt of gratitude to all who contributed to what has become *Leadership: Combat Leaders and Lessons*. One other person deserves special recognition, as well. From the very inception of this project until the manuscript went to the printers, Jim Walsh played a central role. He encouraged Classmates to write and submit, and tirelessly assisted Andy and Jim in every conceivable way. His efforts were indispensable in bringing the project to a successful completion.

What, then, does it all mean? Obviously, that is for you to decide. We, who traveled before you, cannot take your place as you march into the future. The paths you select, the deeds you perform, and the battles you fight will be uniquely yours. All we can offer as a guidepost is the honesty of our experience and the fond hope that one day you, too, will come to look back on your years of service as another worthy chapter in the proud history of the American tradition of arms.

Peter M. Dawkins

Brigadier General, United States Army, Retired

President

INTRODUCTION

In the summer of 2007, a cadet from the West Point Class of 2009 asked the secretary of the Class of 1959 if his classmates would prepare a book of leadership lessons learned – a gift of experience and wisdom for those graduating from the Military Academy fifty years after the secretary's class and about to lead soldiers in the service of our country. Colonel Jim Walsh, USA (Ret.), the class secretary, immediately agreed to take on the task. As he made the long drive home from his visit to the academy, he puzzled with the daunting task of creating a leadership legacy for young leaders wearing cadet gray, one that might also guide soldiers training in Officer Candidate Schools, volunteers of the Reserve Officer Training Corps, and all who prepare to lead American soldiers.

The form that such a guide might take presented another puzzle. A simple listing of leadership principles, even if accompanied by some description, would surely replicate classroom material already presented during officer training. The possibility of a pocket primer for junior officers had somewhat more appeal. Because every section, platoon, company, troop, or battery has its own unique characteristics, branch of service, and traditions, it seemed that no short handbook could provide common responses to unique situations. It would be better to leave that training to the officers' basic course offered by each branch of service.

In the end, a collection of narratives focusing on leadership challenges faced by members of our class seemed the best choice. Reinforced by a few lesser-known events in the careers of some well-known graduates from earlier classes, such accounts could cover the three-decade span of our service at many levels of command. Presented as pieces of personal history, those stories might draw readers into the situations that had once confronted us and encourage young officers to identify with the author and learn from understanding how he applied his education, intelligence, experience, values, and courage in response to a leadership challenge.

Jim Walsh then appealed to members of our class, asking them to take on the tasks of acting as editors and writers in the formulation of a leadership legacy. The class warmly received the challenge, and the two of us, honored by our selection to prepare the collection of leadership lessons, began our work.

The administrative details of assembling input from classmates into a book suitable for publication presented the initial challenge. It soon occurred to us, however, that an introductory comment on the character of leadership, especially combat leadership, was in order. Combat leadership inevitably entails the stuff that makes heroes – troop leading under fire, courage, confidence, perseverance, devotion to duty, integrity, and the close and self-sacrificial bonding that enables military units to succeed in battle.

Even so, we knew our deeds of valor had not truly made us heroes. The heroes of our stories are most often the cherished comrades who fell in battle while performing selfless deeds to protect their buddies and carry out their missions. Such men created indelible memories for each of us as we grieved their loss and surrendered their flag-draped mortal remains to family members. Challenges faced and overcome had also made us better men and better leaders who were more qualified to command the true heroes of our stories.

Preoccupation with heroism is fraught with danger. When leaders begin to see themselves as heroes, they put distance between them and those they lead. They become proud, and in their pride become self-serving. They begin to seek attention for themselves instead of honors for their soldiers. Those seeking recognition as heroes become corrupted leaders and lose the confidence of their troops. Soldiers instinctively sense when the mission and their welfare are no longer uppermost in the mind of a superior entrusted with the command of the unit, an individual who has become corrupted by pursuit of self-promotion. Regrettably, power corrupts; to remain effective, those who lead in battle must remain unselfishly devoted to their duty, their mission, and their troops.

The realization, therefore, emerged as a common consensus that leadership is not the work of heroes. With great humility, our classmates joined us in the task of formulating the lessons of long service in war and peace, in Cold War and hard fought combats, in blizzards, in drenching rains, and in blinding sand storms. Dedication to duty, over many years, has changed all who contributed to this book in ways that enable us to provide valuable insights into the art of leadership. This collection represents our experience as men who did their duty under difficult circumstances. As contributors and editors, we have endeavored to illustrate with words the warrior ethic that bonds soldiers in battle and enables officers to offer leadership that inspires brave young Americans to excel in the most dangerous of circumstances.

Our experience yields a common understanding that our role as leaders was not based on heroism but on solemn responsibility undertaken in the knowledge that we had been entrusted by this great land we love to defend freedom in the face of attacks upon our homeland and loved ones. Our common conviction is that devotion to duty allowed us to show the way as we learned how to encourage often-exhausted soldiers who must prepare and carry out difficult missions even as they felt the grief that accompanies the loss of trusted buddies. In short, our leadership consisted of fidelity to our professional values and putting into practice the motto of our profession and Alma Mater – Duty, Honor, Country.

The Editors
September 5, 2008

ONE
INSPIRATIONAL
LEADERS *from our* PAST

The profession of arms is one of the oldest in human societies.
Long before the written word emerged, ballads and tales of heroism and bold
leaders constituted the traditions that became part of the legacy passed to each new
generation, an inheritance that contributed both to cultural identity and the code of
those who bear arms. Because great military leaders have also placed their stamp
on American society and its profession of arms, we studied their leadership that
we might better understand our society and draw inspiration as we followed in their
noble calling. In the brief chapter that follows, we have recorded some of the words
and deeds of
legendary figures from our nation's past, men whose actions inspired us. As
role models, they guided our quest for service worthy of our traditions and their
examples. Their brave deeds should continue to bear fruit as a new generation
follows in our footsteps.
— The Editors

The Meaning of Responsibility

by Colonel Andrew P. O'Meara, Jr., USA (Ret.)

The following observations on leadership are excerpted from remarks delivered at a graduation ceremony at the Armor School in November 1982.
— The Editors

In the 18th Century, Lord St. Vincent described responsibility as the true test of a man's courage. At Gettysburg in July 1863, Robert E. Lee provided one of the finest American examples of the courage and capacity to accept responsibility. For his 3 July attack on the Union Center – known to history as Pickett's charge – Lee had committed the 11,000 men of the nine brigades in the divisions of Pickett, Pettigrew, and Trimble, which he reinforced with another 1,500 in the brigades commanded by Wilcox and Lane.

Prior to the attack, the Confederate campaign had posed a major threat to Washington. The Confederate States of America had reached their high tide; the Union cause and the Army of the Potomac commanded by George Gordon Meade seemed in grave danger. Though the attackers, ordered by Lee to penetrate the center of Meade's position, got within musket range of their objective, Union forces drove them back with the loss of sixty percent of the Confederate force. The defenders also captured thirty of the thirty-eight regimental flags that came within musket range of the stonewall that marked the Union position.

When the tide broke and the survivors struggled in disorder across the wide valley separating the two armies, Lee's Army, the Army of

Northern Virginia, became the one seriously endangered, reversing the previous roles of the two forces. The attacker now ran a serious risk of being destroyed on Northern soil. More than an attack had failed. The cause of the Confederacy had taken a turn for the worse from which it would never recover. Lee's hopes had been high as he invaded

Major Andrew P. O'Meara, Jr., 11th Armored Calvary, 1968.

Maryland and Pennsylvania. He anticipated victory as the soldiers of Pickett's, Pettigrew's and Trimble's divisions assaulted Cemetery Hill. Observing the attack and seeing it break against the Union center, he moved amongst the survivors as they streamed back across the valley. Fully grasping the dreadful significance of the attackers' failure to break through the Union center, his words help us to understand the meaning of the word responsibility.

Lee met General Pickett with these words, "General Pickett, place your Division in rear of this hill and be ready to repel the advance of the enemy should they follow up their advantage."

Pickett answered tearfully, "General Lee, I have no Division now; Armistead is down, Garnett is down and Kemper is mortally wounded."

"Come, General Pickett," Lee responded. "This has been my fight, and upon my shoulders rests the blame. The men and officers of your command have written the name of Virginia as high today as it has ever been written before. Your men have done all that men can do. The fault is entirely my own." His words later to Wilcox reiterated his total acceptance of responsibility. "It is I who have lost this fight, and you must help me out of it the best way you can."

Responsibility means total acceptance of the men we lead. Their victories are theirs. Their failure is ours – the men who lead them. This is the price of leadership.

Grant's Drive to Richmond

Sergeant Michael J. Faber, USAF (Honorable Discharge)

The quotations attributed to Grant herein are from his letters, dispatches, and personal memoir.
—The Editors

Hiram Ulysses Grant was born in Point Pleasant, Clermont County, Ohio, on 27 April 1822. Arriving at West Point in May of 1839, Grant, concerned that cadets would harass him about his "HUG" initials, decided to change his name to Ulysses H. Grant. The congressman who appointed him, confused about his name, placed his middle name first and inserted his mother's maiden name (Simpson). From that point on, he was known as Ulysses S. Grant and called "U.S. Grant," "Uncle Sam" or just "Sam" by his fellow cadets and later by his fellow officers.

The young Grant had no illusions of grandeur about life as an Army officer. "A military life had no charms for me, and I had not the faintest idea of staying in the Army even if I should be graduated, which I did not expect." Despite that expectation, Grant graduated from West Point in June 1843, ranked 21st in a class of 39. He distinguished himself in the Mexican War, and the Army next assigned him, without his family, to Fort Vancouver, Oregon. Though promoted to captain in 1853, he resigned from the Army and returned to St. Louis when accused of excessive drinking. Struggling as a farmer and tanner and eventually working as a clerk in his father's leather goods store in Galena, Illinois,

Grant's outlook appeared dismal as 1860 came to a close.

With the Civil War suddenly looming, however, Grant decided to return to the Army, and in May of 1861 he began actively seeking a commission. In a letter to Adjutant General Lorenzo Thomas, Grant wrote, "I feel myself competant [*sic*] to command a regiment if the President, in his judgement [*sic*], should see fit to entrust one to me." General Thomas never answered the letter. The next month, Grant visited the Cincinnati headquarters of George B. McClellan to seek a staff appointment, but McClellan refused to receive him. Persevering in the face of disappointment, Grant finally accepted from Illinois Governor Richard Yates the offer of a commission as colonel of the Seventh District Regiment.

It must have been a tremendous blow to Grant when McClellan refused to meet with him in St. Louis and his letters went unanswered. With a tarnished reputation and his recent struggles, it would have been easy to yield to self-pity and give up. Believing in himself and in his ability to lead, Grant continued to pursue his goal of re-entering the Army. Taking command of the unruly and rebellious Seventh District Regiment might not have been his preferred choice, but it achieved his goal of returning to the Army in a leadership position.

Grant's military successes in the West (including victories at Belmont, Henry, Donelson, Vicksburg and Chattanooga) proved his detractors wrong and propelled Grant to command of all Union forces in the western theater. His collaboration and friendship with William Tecumseh Sherman are the subject of an excellent 2005 book by Charles Bracelen Flood, *Grant and Sherman: The Friendship That Won The Civil War.*

His triumph in the west led Grant to his biggest challenge. On 8 March 1864, Lincoln and Grant met in person for the first time. Following recent legislation to restore the rank of lieutenant general,

Grant received his third star, and Lincoln gave him command of all armies of the United States. That evening, in his brief acceptance speech, Grant was modest and to the point: "Mr. President, I accept the commission, with gratitude for the high honor conferred. With the aid of the noble armies that have fought in so many fields for our common country, it will be my earnest endeavor not to disappoint your expectations. I feel the full weight of the responsibilities now devolving on me, and I know that if they are met, it will be due to those armies, and above all, to the favor of that Providence which leads both nations and men."

Grant remained modest, stayed focused on the challenge at hand, and often remembered and thanked his soldiers for the sacrifices they were making. Unlike many of the politically motivated generals who had preceded him, Grant carefully avoided the pitfalls of politics and until after the war kept focused on military matters.

Grant appointed Sherman to take his place as commander in Nashville and made his headquarters with the Army of the Potomac still commanded by George Meade. With those actions, he had set the stage for the epic confrontation between Robert E. Lee's Army of Northern Virginia and the Army of the Potomac. In previous Virginia battles, Grant's predecessors had retreated after major confrontations. Rejecting that behavior, he chose relentlessly to push the offensive, forcing Lee to remain on defense and giving him no opportunity to regroup, re-supply, and regain the initiative.

In what became known as Grant's Overland Campaign, the 5 to 7 May Battle of the Wilderness marked the first major confrontation between Lee and Grant. In the area's heavy undergrowth, both sides suffered horrendous casualties, and many of the battle-weary Union soldiers expected Grant to pull back as previous commanders had done. When Grant, instead, ordered his men to advance to the southeast around Lee's left flank, his soldiers, especially the veterans who had fought so hard in previous Virginia battles only to later relinquish their gains, greeted the decision to advance with overwhelming approval.

In spite of significant losses, Grant stayed with his plan to press the attack. He was determined to wear down and destroy Lee's army and thereby end the Civil War. Fighting resumed at Spotsylvania on 8 May and raged for fourteen days. During this fighting, Grant wrote his famous dispatch to General Halleck: "I propose to fight it out on this line if it takes all Summer." On 12 May, Grant ordered Hancock's 2nd Corps to attack Lee's line. Hancock broke through, capturing 4,000 Confederate prisoners and thirty artillery pieces. The momentum began to turn in Grant's favor.

Then disaster struck. On 3 June Grant ordered a massive three-corps attack on a well-defended Confederate position at Cold Harbor. In what became one of Grant's most controversial decisions, opponents criticized him for attacking such a strongly defended position and for lack of adequate reconnaissance prior to the attack. The attack cost the Union an estimated 3,000-7,000 killed, wounded, and missing in the first forty minutes (modern estimates lean towards the lower number). Regardless of the precise number, Grant sincerely regretted the last assault at Cold Harbor. In his *Personal Memoirs of U.S. Grant*, he later wrote: "I have always regretted that the last assault at Cold Harbor was ever made. I might say the same thing of the assault of the 22nd May, 1863 [*sic*] at Vicksburg. At Cold Harbor no advantage whatever was gained to compensate for the heavy loss we sustained."

Sergeant Michael J. Faber, USAF (Honorary Member Class of 1959).

Despite the horrendous losses at Cold Harbor and his regrets

7

and disappointment with his conduct of the battle, Grant continued to press the attack against Lee. He also accepted full responsibility for losses at Cold Harbor and other engagements of the campaign. By mid-June, Grant's army had moved across the James River headed towards Petersburg. With Grant unable to break through Lee's lines, Petersburg settled into a siege. In a failed attempt to break it, on 30 July the Union Army exploded a huge underground mine beneath Confederate fortifications, but the planned follow-up attack ended in complete disaster. General Ambrose Burnside failed to plan the follow-up attack properly, and his subordinate, General James Ledlie, hid in the rear while Confederate riflemen slaughtered his troops.

Grant later wrote of the failure at the Battle of the Crater: "I think the cause of the disaster was simply leaving the passage of orders from one to another down to an inefficient man. I blame his seniors also for not seeing that he did his duty, all the way up to myself." Grant was obviously furious over the lack of coordination following the mine explosion, but he had the humility to include himself in the criticism. Again, Grant accepted total responsibility, this time for the lack of success at the Battle of the Crater.

The next spring, surrounded and out of military options, General Robert E. Lee had no choice but to surrender to Grant at Appomattox. Grant's civility, professionalism, and respect for Lee and his men set the stage for ending hostilities and the beginning of a difficult period of reconstruction following the Civil War. Someone without General Ulysses S. Grant's calm and thoughtful demeanor could easily have triggered months or even years of Confederate guerrilla resistance.

Writing about Grant's leadership qualities in his *Ulysses S. Grant: The Unlikely Hero*, historian Michael Korda observed: "Grant understood topography, the importance of supply lines, the instant judgment of the balance between his own strengths and the enemy's weaknesses, and above all the need to keep his armies moving forward, despite casualties, even when things had gone wrong – that and the simple importance of inflicting greater losses on the enemy than he can sustain, day after day, until he breaks. Grant the boy never retraced his steps. Grant the man did not retreat – he advanced. Generals who do that win wars."

The Savage Wars of Peace

by Colonel James L. Abrahamson, USA (Ret.)

Overlooking the poorly understood war in Vietnam, many Americans wrongly believe that the conflicts in Iraq and Afghanistan represent the first wars in which the United States Government called upon its Soldiers and Marines to perform so-called "nation building" tasks for which their training had not formally prepared them. Based upon Black Jack, *Frank E. Vandiver's biography of John J. Pershing, who later commanded U. S. ground forces in World War I, this summary of Pershing's 1909-1913 service in the Philippines should make clear that lack of formal training need not prevent officers from effectively accomplishing tasks that merit description as political, economic, and social even as they demonstrate personal courage in battles against those who threaten their command's security. The American armed forces have long served ably in what Rudyard Kipling in "The White Man's Burden" called the savage wars of peace.*

– The Editors

Having already served four years in the Philippine Islands at the conclusion of the Spanish-American War, new-Brigadier General John J. Pershing returned to the Islands in November 1909. This time he commanded the military Department of Mindanao as well as serving as the military governor of the Islands' Moro Province. He thus became responsible for the thirty thousand square miles of land in a group of islands constituting a third of America's new colony in the Western Pacific. Assisted by a small civil staff, a constabulary police force, local courts, and his four-man Legislative Council, which he chaired, Pershing governed the province through five commissioned district governors. Just over five thousand troops, mostly U. S. regulars, made up his military command.

Inhabited mostly by Muslim Moros, the province also included Christian Filipinos, Chinese merchants, and a small number of Europeans and Americans. The Filipinos feared the violent Moros, who hated all Christians, especially Filipino Christians. The Chinese strove to remain neutral and stick to business. Despite immediate postwar efforts to pacify the province, in which Pershing had previously played a part, he soon learned that in 1909 large numbers of the well-armed Moros still terrorized the population by piracy, slavery, kidnapping, and murder. Development and local self-government, "nation building" in modern parlance, could not progress well until the rebels amongst the Moros had laid down their weapons.

Averse to bloody battles that killed more non-combatants than armed rebels, Pershing hoped to accomplish the Moros' disarmament by winning the hearts and minds of his subjects. He would do this through gentle persuasion and by reforming his province's economic and social systems, thereby reducing poverty and sloth and giving the population reasons to support the American administration. To that end, he sorted out the province's archaic and chaotic system of land ownership and soon began settling families on farms to which they held secure legal title. He also introduced new farming methods and such new food crops as corn and potatoes while promoting the recovery of sugar cane, hemp, and others of the province's commercial plantation crops.

As tax revenues permitted, Pershing improved the province's health clinics and facilitated commerce by extending roads, telephone, and telegraph lines that gave remote areas access to up-graded port facilities. Dedicated American schoolteachers and the Filipinos they trained enabled Pershing gradually to reform the schools and their curricula.

Whenever possible, the governor also awarded government positions to peaceful Moro leaders, those who consented to the surrender of their followers' guns and all their long non-agricultural knives. In return, the provincial constabulary and its companies of American-trained Filipino and Moro Scouts, backed up by U. S. regulars, faced the challenge of securing the peaceful population and disarming all those who wished to continue the old and violent practices of the past — a significant test considering the extent of the province, its many islands, and the small size of the security forces.

Two areas posed the principal threat to the peace of Moro Province: Moro rebels in and around Lake Lanao near the center of the large island of Mindanao and those on much smaller Jolo in the Sulu Archipelago. In each place, persuasion and reconstruction had faltered, and Pershing eventually found it necessary to wage Rudyard Kipling's "savage wars of peace" and to do so with minimal casualties to both the hostile non-combatant population as well as his small military force of regulars and U. S. trained local troops. Those battles would also be fought in an American presidential election year under the eye of a generally hypercritical press, politicians concerned about civilian casualties in an increasingly unpopular war, and a few figures in the War Department eager to see Pershing fail. Do some things never change?

Pershing left the disarmament of Lanao's rebels to his district military governor and the U. S. regulars under his command. Though too slowly, pacification moved forward there.

ɔlo was another matter, one requiring the general's personal
:ion. Under Colonel Frank West, Pershing formed the Jolo Field
Forces consisting of two squadrons of cavalry, a regiment of infantry,
a battalion of field artillery, six
companies of scouts, and two of
constabulary. Pershing sent that
force against about 250 warriors
likely to gather in the fortifications
on Bud Dajo, an extinct volcano
in western Jolo. The local Moros
regarded this as a sacred site, their
last bastion, and the place from

*Colonel
James L.
Abraham-
son, USA
(Ret.).*

which they would likely fight to the death. Though West's forces could
surely overcome the warriors, what would be the fate of the five to
eight hundred women and children who would join their men folk in
the cottas (fortifications)? Pershing opposed and could hardly afford a
slaughter of civilians.

Realizing that he had committed his forces so quickly that the
Moros had little time to stock their fortification with supplies for a long
siege, Pershing ordered his troops to surround the mountain and after
a personal reconnaissance, concentrated his forces where they could
prevent supplies from reaching the Moros on its fortified peak. While
the troops patrolled rather than assaulted, small parties of hungry Moros
began surrendering. The numbers soon increased, and within weeks,
resistance had collapsed in that part of Jolo. Pershing's losses were only
one U. S. officer and two scouts; only twelve Moro warriors died.

Although Pershing then left Jolo to attend to his duties as provincial
governor, disarmament went smoothly, except in Lati Ward in the
island's center. In that ward, Datto Amil led the resistance from extensive
fortifications around another extinct volcano, Mt. Bagsak. Whenever

U. S. forces entered the ward, its Moro population — men, women, and children — raced to the mountain's well-stocked cottas. Though Amil negotiated, he refused to disarm and continued to raid the area even as he talked. Direct bloody assault on the fortifications seemed out of the question until Pershing could separate the violent ten percent of the ward's population from the ninety percent of its innocent non-combatants.

Once again Pershing went to Jolo and soon reached a deal with Amir: The Americans would leave the ward and the Moros would return home to plant their crops rather than raid. The general withdrew his troops. Moro women, children, and a few unarmed men left the mountain to plant, but Amil's forces resumed their violence. When they attacked Augur Barracks in Jolo City, Pershing had had enough of talking, as had the editors of the *Manila Times*, who berated Pershing for allowing the Moro rebels to scream "defiance at the white man." He was, the newsmen concluded, no fighter. In fact, the general had a plan.

Detaching regulars from the Jolo garrison and ordering the remaining units to cease field operations, Pershing seemed to turn his back on the island and sail away. Back on Mindanao, he announced plans to visit his family. Ostentatiously boarding the *Wright*, he sailed away only to bring the ship about and race toward Jolo when out of sight of land, picking up companies of Moro Scouts en route. Returning to Jolo harbor at night, he issued orders for the concentration of the island's other forces — a troop of cavalry, several more companies of scouts, and two mountain gun contingents. By land and sea, Pershing's gathering forces raced for Bagsak to ensure that no non-combatants or additional insurgents reached its fortifications. He achieved complete surprise, and only a few hundred hostiles occupied the mountain.

After advancing within a mile of the mountain's top, Pershing dispersed his forces to launch simultaneous attacks on three mutually supporting cottas whose capture would leave the other fortifications isolated and left to fight alone. With the support of a mountain gun and rifle fire from the units heading toward the third fort, the ground assaults on the first two forts quickly overcame their resistance with the loss of only five scouts. Taking a concealed route that took them around and above the third fort, two companies of scouts surprised its defenders and seized the fort with but five wounded scouts. The Moros soon abandoned several of the lesser cottas.

The next day, Pershing directed his artillery against the principal remaining fort atop Bagsak, where the Moro leader, Datto Amil, lay wounded from the previous day's battles. His death during the bombardment undermined the Moros' morale but not their determination to die a martyr's death. In an effort to silence the guns reducing their fort to rubble, they donned their finest clothes and launched waves of suicidal attacks on Pershing's scouts, whose disciplined fire cut gaps in their lines.

Looking for a better route to the top of Bagsak, Pershing ordered an attack on a poorly defended cotta, made a personal reconnaissance that carried him within 75 yards of the cotta atop the mountain, and then shifted his artillery to support a final assault the next day. The battle pitted American-trained Moro Scouts against Moro insurgents. Distressed by the earlier death of one of his officers, Pershing ordered the scouts' Moro non-commissioned officers to direct the attack. After taking the first trench line, however, the attack bogged down. Pershing went to the front to encourage his scouts and consolidate their position. He also ordered his American officers back into the line. As expected, the Moro insurgents counter-attacked, and the scouts repulsed them with heavy losses. As his scouts surged forward in pursuit, Pershing caught the spirit, and with pistol drawn, he joined the vanguard for the final assault on the fort.

Though fourteen scouts and one American officer lay dead, Pershing estimated the casualties of the Moro defenders at between two and three hundred with another hundred fled or captured. With Moro resistance on Jolo now completely broken, the island's pacification could succeed.

For what biographer Vandiver called Pershing's "reckless personal exposure" at the climax of the hard fought battle, several of the general's officers and enlisted men submitted certificates calling on the Army to award him the Medal of Honor. Dissatisfied with the way he had divided rather than concentrated his forces, misjudged the need to keep his American officers with their units throughout the attack, as well as the necessity for his personal intervention at the decisive moment, Pershing told the Army's Adjutant General that he did not deserve the award. For the success of the attack, he credited the magnificent performance of all but one of the U. S. trained scout companies.

When Pershing departed the Philippines for the second time in December 1913, he left a disarmed and peaceful province with a strong provincial government sustained by a growing economy, an improved infrastructure, and a reformed educational system. Emphasizing disarmament through persuasion and, when that failed, fighting battles that caused few non-combatant deaths ensured that Pershing's administration retained the support he had gained by visiting all parts of his province, seeking out and patiently listening to the residents of Moroland: the small farmers; Filipino workers; Chinese merchants; Moro leaders; and European planters.

When force seemed the only means to achieve disarmament and put an end to violent mayhem, the general skillfully moved his units of U. S. regulars and local scouts to overcome those who threatened the peace of the province, even when that required him to save the day with a show of personal courage. Though West Point had not taught its graduates how to build nations, Pershing demonstrated they could triumph in both the civil and military struggles of the "savage wars of peace," even in the face of criticism from the press and the home front.

Inspirational Leadership in the Trenches
by Colonel James L. Abrahamson, USA (Ret.)

Following the 16 April 1917 American declaration of war on Germany, President Woodrow Wilson faced important questions about the nature and extent of his nation's commitment to the war. Would he vastly expand and make official the financial and material support already flowing from private sources to his new French and British allies? Would he commit the powerful U. S. Navy to back up Allied, especially British, control of the seas and thereby help block German and Austrian access to international trade, keep the naval powers of the Central Powers bottled up in their home ports, and wage war on the German submarines seeking to limit Allied access to American suppliers? Would he, in addition, commit American land forces to the bloody stalemate in northern France? If so, what would be the size and organization of that force?

Regarding ground forces, the Army's General Staff initially recommended a limited commitment to the land battle, a less than a three-fold expansion of the Regular Army. As a major serving on the General Staff, Douglas MacArthur rather too brusquely added to that staff study his opposition to a commitment of only a half million men, all of them Regulars. When Chief of Staff Hugh Scott approved that study, MacArthur expected a reprimand for his rash behavior. Instead, Secretary of War Newton D. Baker soon asked to see the bold young major, expressed agreement with his views, and told him to grab his hat as the two men headed for the White House to speak with President Woodrow Wilson.

A presidential decision eliminated the proposed limit on the United States commitment of land forces and included the National Guard in the plans for the Army's expansion. Based upon MacArthur's notion of uniting the country behind the war effort by drawing divisional components from National Guard units in twenty-six states–a rainbow stretching from California to New York and from Alabama to Minnesota–the 42nd "Rainbow" Division became early fruit of the new policy. After Baker named Brigadier General William A. Mann, Chief of the Militia Bureau, an officer nearing retirement, to command that new division, he asked MacArthur what remained to be done. When the major urged Baker to assign the Army's best colonel as the division's chief of staff, the Secretary told MacArthur he had already selected him for that position and promptly signed orders promoting him to colonel.

Thereafter, MacArthur's extraordinary and heroic service in World War I, sketched below, became an inseparable part of both his biography and the division's history. The following account of MacArthur's leadership and exploits draws upon two of his books, Reminiscences *and* Courage Was the Rule, *which are also the sources of all quoted passages.*

– The Editors

Once assembled on Long Island, units of the 42nd Infantry Division trained for two months before sailing for France in mid-October 1917. There it received its artillery and, eventually based near Rolampont in the Meuse River valley, continued preparations for entering the fight. During the training of American divisions already in France, General John J. Pershing, Commander-in-Chief of the American Expeditionary Force, struggled with his Allies. They wished to integrate his soldiers into existing French or British formations, which would have prevented the creation of an independent American Army holding a sector of the Allied front lines. On that, both Pershing and President Wilson insisted. Nevertheless, for training purposes and when the Germans pressed his allies particularly hard, Pershing did agree to send small units and individual divisions to replace allied formations needed to counter German advances.

In February 1918, Pershing moved the Rainbow Division to the Luneville-Baccarat area then held by the French VII Corps, commanded by General Georges de Bazelaire. The U. S. commander-in-chief also named Major General Charles T. Menoher to assume command of the 42nd. MacArthur soon learned that Menoher, a former field artilleryman, preferred to direct the division from his command headquarters while his chief of staff commanded the battle line, an unusual arrangement that nevertheless suited MacArthur's personality and desires.

When the division assigned its four infantry regiments, one each, to the four divisions of the French Corps, MacArthur demonstrated his eagerness to examine, at first hand, the enemy that the regiments would soon face. With great reluctance, the French corps commander allowed the American colonel to accompany a French raiding party seeking to test the Germans' lines and capture prisoners as a means to gain intelligence. To win the French general's approval, MacArthur told him: "I cannot fight them if I cannot see them."

With blackened faces, MacArthur and the French soldiers made their way through the barbed wire and war refuse of the no man's land between the trench lines. As the party neared its objective, the Germans discovered its presence, fired flares, roused the trench line, which took it under fire, and commenced an artillery barrage that cut off the party's line of retreat. In what MacArthur described as a "savage and merciless" fight, the raiding party nevertheless gained control of a section of the

German trenches and seized several prisoners before returning to French lines. The American colonel had so impressed the French with his courage that he immediately became "one of them," and Bazelaire promptly pinned the Croix de Guerre on MacArthur's tunic. He would soon thereafter receive the first of his seven Silver Stars.

By March, the 42nd Division's units had turned back an enemy raid and a night gas attack and successfully performed the trench duties of a unit in defense. The time had come to see how well the Americans—in this case a battalion of the 168th Infantry Regiment—would perform when directed to seize a section of the German trench line in the Salient du Feys. When the battalion went over the top at 0505, MacArthur went with it and immediately felt the fiery blast of the friendly artillery falling on the German lines. For a few seconds, he wondered if the men were following him. In a moment of great pride, he soon discovered that "they were around me, ahead of me, a roaring avalanche of glittering steel and cursing men. We carried the enemy position." The 42nd had made its reputation, and MacArthur received the first of two Distinguished Service Crosses he would receive during the First World War.

In the spring of 1918, the Germans, reinforcing their forces in the West after Russia made a separate peace, sought to knock the British and French out of the war before the American Army became fully prepared. Responding to a series of great offensives, the French withdrew many of their units to block an assault aimed at Paris and consequently left the 42nd to defend the entire Baccarat section of the Lorraine front during more than eighty days of constant combat. Before the division left the sector, the commander of the French VI Corps, under which the division had fought with such skill, personally praised MacArthur and predicted that the division would "henceforth take a glorious place in the new line of battle."

The division received little rest. On 4 July, after intelligence revealed that the group of armies commanded by the German Crown Prince planned an attack designed to split the British and French forces in Champagne, the Allied high command sent the 42nd to become part of the French Fourth Army commanded by General Henri Gouraud. The French general had worked out a new theory of defense that MacArthur quickly embraced — a defense in depth that created a death trap for the attacker. In anticipation of receiving a major attack, the defenders would evacuate their front line positions, leaving behind only a few "suicide squads" to detect the start of the German advance and fire rockets to alert forces in a secondary trench line, which had become the new main line of resistance. Upon reaching the evacuated trenches, the Germans, believing they had achieved an easy success, would move rapidly forward. At that point, the defenders would take them under heavy fire to destroy their momentum and render them a spent force before they reached the defenders holding the new line of defense.

When the capture of a Prussian officer revealed the expected German attack would begin shortly after midnight on 15 July, General Gouraud ordered his artillery force of a thousand guns to begin firing forty minutes before midnight. Caught by surprise and under an artillery attack that disrupted their movements, the Germans became disconcerted even before their infantry reached the trench line the French and Americans had evacuated in accord with the new tactics. Watching from the new main line of defense, MacArthur observed the division's skillful use of the new tactics as its heavy fire exhausted the attackers and broke their formations even before they reached the division's front line. Counter attacks soon turned back the German forces, bringing to an end their last great offensive. General Gauraud lavishly praised the courage of the men of the Rainbow Division and the skill with which they had employed the new tactics. For his role, MacArthur received his second Silver Star.

With the strategic initiative now passing to the allies, the Rainbow Division once again shifted its front, this time to the sector occupied by General Jean Degoutte's Sixth Army, where it relieved the exhausted U. S. 26th "Yankee" Division, another National Guard unit, on 25 July. As the Germans fell back from their recent defeat, they left behind machine gun and mortar parties that bitterly contested the Rainbow Division's advance. On the offense, MacArthur once again changed the division's tactics. During six days of often hand-to-hand combat, the Guardsmen crawled forward in twos and threes, as in the Indian wars, and used bayonets and hand grenades to silence each machine gun and mortar before being taken under fire from the next German strong point.

Shortly after midnight on 30 July, MacAthur, reconnoitering in front of the division's outposts, detected sounds indicating the Germans might be withdrawing. Acting on his own initiative in order to seize the advantage, he traversed the division's four-kilometer front, a rugged trip in the dark of night through the former no man's land, to direct that each regiment prepare to advance with one battalion on line, followed by a second in support, and a third in column. At the appointed time, they were to move out simultaneously. He then went to division headquarters, where he announced his plan. Not having slept for four days, he thereafter collapsed in sleep. The division, led by its engineer regiment acting as infantry, moved forward according to the plans MacArthur had made. The Germans, denied time to reorganize, fell back as far as the Vesle River before they could make a new stand. For his initiative and daring, he won a second Croix de Guerre from the French, his fourth Silver Star, and promotion to brigadier general and command of Rainbow's 84th Infantry Brigade. The division's former chief of staff now had even more reason to continue commanding from the front.

In August, after receiving replacements and re-supply, the division moved to the St. Mihiel salient, where it became part of the IV Corps of the newly formed American First Army. On 10 September MacArthur led his brigade in the attack for the first time. Having observed the Germans' habits for some time, he knew their tendency to concentrate forces so as to protect the center of their line even as this weakened its flanks. He therefore directed his regiments to pierce both flanks and then begin to envelop the Germans' center, which sent them into a rapid retreat. By the end of the day, the brigade had broken through to the plain that stretched as far as Metz, a fortress and transportation center that the Germans must hold in order to supply their forces and for the U. S. a jumping off point for a possible allied invasion of central Germany. The next day, MacArthur pushed his brigade within twenty kilometers of Metz and became convinced, through a nighttime personal reconnaissance to the outskirts of the city, that the Germans had, for the moment, left the immense fortress largely undefended. His forceful recommendation for an immediate attack received support at division, corps, and army level, but the U. S. high command had made other plans and refused to seize an unexpected opportunity. Soon thereafter, the Germans reoccupied the Metz fortress.

By the first of October, the 42nd had again relocated, this time to join the eighty-mile Meuse-Argonne front where a million-man American Army had already begun its attempt to break through the strongly defended center of the German front in northern France. Should that offensive reach Sedan, it would collapse the Hindenburg Line and likely force Germany's surrender. By the time the Rainbow Division had arrived, several other American divisions had already been thrown back with dreadful losses when they tried to overcome the key to the German defenses. Directed to replace the bloodied 1st Division, the first unit to reach France and the pride of the Regular forces, MacArthur realized what others had not, the division could not advance until it had first taken the Cote-de-Chatillon. When the V Corps commander, Major General Charles P. Summerall, called on MacArthur at his command post the night of 11 October, the new brigadier rashly promised either to take Chatillon or know his name would head the list of casualties.

Slightly wounded while making a reconnaissance, MacArthur again observed the Germans' preference for strengthening their center at the expense of their flanks. He therefore sent his regiment of Alabamans to the left and his regiment of Iowans to the right and planned to use every available machine gun and artillery piece to provide covering fire. Moving out on a misty dawn, his troops crawled from one bit of cover to the next only to quickly form as a squad or platoon when needed to overcome some point of resistance. By nightfall the Iowans had occupied their objective. After some readjustments, the next day the brigade seized another key part of Chatillon's defenses and skirted around a third. Though the attackers suffered extremely heavy losses, the last defenses of the German position fell when two of the brigade's battalions closed on it in a pincer movement. Summerall cited the brigade's Guardsmen for the "highest soldierly qualities" and "services of the greatest valor" and for displaying in the face of fierce German resistance a "dash, courage and fighting spirit worthy of the best traditions of the American Army." The brigade's commanding officer received his second Distinguished Service Cross and a recommendation for promotion to major general.

* * * * *

As chief of staff and brigade commander, MacArthur had never failed to lead his Guardsmen from their front lines, often going forward of their positions to seek information essential to the success of their operations. Typically wearing no helmet, as it hurt his head, carrying no gas mask, as it hindered his movement, and "armed" only with a riding crop, as his job was to command not fire a weapon, he always fought from the front as that was the best location from which to direct the movement of his units. When some of MacArthur's peers made such behavior a matter of an official complaint referred to General Pershing, the commander in chief exploded: "Stop all this nonsense. MacArthur is the greatest leader of troops we have, and I intend to make him a divisional commander."

The armistice of 11 November blocked that promotion, but it could not diminish the courage and leadership qualities that MacArthur had displayed during his service in France: Commanding from the front, he always moved close enough to understand his enemy, detect his weaknesses, and maneuver his own forces to exploit them. Whether attacking or defending, he repeatedly showed initiative and adjusted his tactics as demanded by the situation. For both the Guardsmen and their officers he set an extraordinary example of personal courage. Small wonder that Pershing had such great regard for the brilliance and valor of Douglas MacArthur's leadership.

Genius and the Art of War

by Colonel Andrew P. O'Meara, Jr., USA (Ret.)

Genius lives in a cognitive world beyond the pale, far removed from the ken of the learned of its time. Genius treads upon unknown ground. Its essence is the capacity to operate, to think and translate thought into action beyond the limits of contemporary understanding. Great genius explores new cognitive ground and opens doors that others might see beyond the

24

previous limits of human knowledge, allowing lesser men to accompany genius by articulating insights into practical concepts that expand the horizons of human understanding.

The following account of General Patton's leadership and exploits draws upon two books, Eisenhower's Lieutenants *by Russell F. Weigley and* Warrior: The Story of General George S. Patton, Jr. *by the Editors of the* Army Times, *which are also the sources of all quoted passages.*
—The Editors

The origin of genius resides in understanding the limits of knowledge in established disciplines or art. It becomes manifest by making the plunge into abstract thought articulating concepts that permit men to follow where none have theretofore trod. Operating beyond the limits of human understanding, genius is accompanied by the possibility of great error. On unknown philosophical ground where practical experience remains as yet untried, the difficulty becomes differentiating between truth and error, or more importantly between the useful and the destructive. As a result, the great thinkers of every age accept the risks and the responsibility for their giant leaps into the unknown. Einstein plunged into the unknown world beyond what scientists knew of Quantum Physics to revolutionize science by publishing his Theory of Relativity. Having done so, he posited experiments to validate his theory. He offered precise tests to the scientific community that would one day establish the validity or demonstrate the fallacy of his theory. He then stepped back and allowed others to test his new and revolutionary scientific concepts.

Regrettably, not all innovators are so responsible. Genius sometimes fails to seek altruistic ends. Some rely on genius to pursue ends that are self-serving and corrupt the science they feign to serve. Irresponsible theorists transcend the limits of human knowledge, establishing false premises and refusing to acknowledge failure by altering theory when confronted by contradictions between predicted and observed behavior. Karl Marx and his followers were such men. They altered his theory, rewrote history and consistently denied failure even when failure stalked them. Men such as Karl Marx and Adolph Hitler wrote innovative works that mobilized mass movements to implement their theories through war, revolution, and seizure of power. Placing self-aggrandizement and power seizure above the common good, they propagated untested and destructive manifestos that resulted in unprecedented suffering and genocide. The lessons are that genius is unpredictable and innovative thought that transcends practical experience requires validation.

The art of war has seen many geniuses – men such as Alexander the Great, Napoleon Bonaparte, Sun Tzu, and Robert E. Lee. These men enjoyed total mastery of the state of the art. They recognized the character of both the battlefield and their opponents and elected to operate in unique patterns, innovating tactics and strategies in the process. Napoleon documented his methods by writing his *Maxims of War*, while Sun Tzu wrote the *Art of War* to permit others to understand his methods. The lesson here is that, in addition to validating untried concepts, teaching subordinates to understand innovative ideas is essential to the application of new methods.

Among military geniuses, General George S. Patton was among the foremost during World War II. The case can be made that other leaders in the war also possessed genius, but Patton stands alone as the most successful proponent of tactical exploitation on the battlefield. His successes rested upon innovation and audacity. A student of history and the art of war, Patton understood his German opponents, their methods of waging war – *Blitzkrieg* – as well as their operational limits. Understanding his own army and that of his opponents, he chose to operate beyond the limits of German capabilities. He did so by relying upon the technical advantages of the American armed forces of World War II, while effectively nullifying the strengths of the *Wehrmacht*. In addition, he took calculated risks that placed his forces in position to exploit German limitations.

The Germans were quick to recognize Patton's brilliance. They observed his operations in North Africa and in Sicily, where he outmaneuvered and destroyed his opponents by relentless pressure, envelopment, rapid exploitation, and the devastating combined firepower of air, sea, and ground forces. Patton's achievements fully exploited the mobility and superior logistics enjoyed by American armed forces, which the Germans could not hope to match. Patton's flare for leadership drove his units to achieve remarkable successes in North Africa and Sicily, despite the fact that his demands for excellence and his intolerance of cowardice resulted in two slapping incidents involving soldiers suffering from battle fatigue. These actions hurt his reputation and nearly cost him the opportunity to command the Third Army in France. Fortunately, Patton learned from his errors and went on to lead Third Army, the most effective army of its day, to defeat armies of the Third Reich and hasten the conquest of Gross Deutschland.

What did Patton recognize about the state of the armies that allowed him to inflict ruinous defeats upon his opponents? Unlike the standardized structure of the American Army, the German Army was a hybrid force. The vast majority of the *Wehrmacht* employed technologies and logistics used in World War I – dismounted infantry that marched into battle carrying the Mauser rifle supplied by horse drawn wagons, and heavily reliant upon rail transport to sustain their military operations – a mode of transportation soon systematically destroyed by air interdiction. The World War I technology of the German infantry and supply services was wedded to a smaller but highly mobile corps of assault formations composed of air and ground forces that spearheaded the German invasions of Poland, France, and the Soviet Union.

The German *Blitzkreig*, or lightning war, was conducted by mobile formations using innovative assault tactics executed by specialized German forces made up of the *Waffen SS*, Panzer formations, and the *Luftwaffe*, or air force. Following the Normandy invasion, however, the Luftwaffe ceased to play a major role in the final battles of the war. German flyers who survived the early air battles of the war largely focused on the defense of German industrial targets against massive Allied bomber raids. The result of the urgent need to protect German industry from air attacks meant that a key player in the early successes of the *Blitzkreig* invariably went missing from the German combined arms team in the final year of the war. American and British ground forces consequently enjoyed air superiority during the majority of their campaigns in the European Theater of War.

The German Panzer troops enjoyed substantial advantages in tank and anti-tank guns over their allied opponents. Built for mobility, and sacrificing armor protection to achieve it, the American M-4 Sherman and the British tanks of the period relied upon low muzzle velocity 75-mm guns. The German Tiger tank had a high velocity 75-mm gun that could easily destroy a Sherman tank with a frontal hit, whereas the Sherman's armor-piercing rounds bounced off the frontal armor of the Tiger tank. To negate the German advantages in high velocity anti-tank guns, the American tankers depended upon flank shots as well as close air support and massed artillery fires.

Taken as a whole, the German army very nearly matched the allied forces in the bitter warfare that confronted the American forces in the hedgerows following the Normandy invasion, despite the fact that the Germans became outnumbered as American reinforcements continued to enter the conflict. Both armies sustained heavy losses in the battles of the hedgerows. Exhausted by the bitter fighting in the Bocage country, the commander of the German LXXXIV Corps, General von Cholitz, described the action as "one tremendous bloodbath, such as I have never seen in eleven years of war." Despite their losses, the German army put up a determined fight in the hedgerows.

The Germans could not, however, match the mobility of the American forces, which put them at a substantial disadvantage when confronted by the fast-moving maneuver warfare that Patton waged. Breaking out of the Normandy beachhead, he quickly recognized that he could attack much more rapidly than the Germans could withdraw. The mobility of his forces and the daring exploits he led overwhelmed the German High Command and left his less mobile opponents in confusion and near panic as they sought to escape bypassed battle positions in danger of being cut off by the deep attacks of the Americans. Forced to take to the roads to escape encirclement, German tanks, artillery, and infantry became easy targets for allied air cover that dominated the battlefield.

The Normandy invasion took place on 6 June 1944. On the left the British Second Army rapidly secured its beachheads, despite the fact that stubborn German resistance halted the British advance short of Caen – its D-Day objective. The American invasion forces of First Army, under the command of General Bradley, encountered stiff opposition at Omaha Beach and sustained heavy casualties, whereas the landings at Utah Beach achieved their initial objectives with far fewer casualties. By 12 June the Americans had taken their D-Day objectives, pushing inland into a Norman countryside broken up by the hedgerows stubbornly defended by the Germans.

By 20 June the American VII Corps, under the command of General Collins, had overrun the Cotentin peninsula and on 27 June captured Cherbourg. By 30 June the American advance had secured its objectives along a front that stretched from the west coast of the Cotentin peninsula to link up with the embattled British Second Army still short of its D-Day objective. Relentless attacks along the entire front finally resulted in the capture of Caen by the British on 24 July, while General Bradley's expanded First Army, attacking with four corps abreast, succeeded in pushing through the worst of the hedgerows of the Norman countryside to capture St. Lo. Given the lack of success by the British in forcing a breakthrough in the open country on the left of the allied line, the American forces prepared for a major push to break the German defenses on the allied right flank at St. Lo. General Bradley directed an aerial bombardment of the German defenses followed by the breakout to commence a major push to secure the ports of the Brittany Peninsula and envelop the German Seventh Army facing the allied invasion forces securing the Normandy coast.

The rapid buildup of American forces allowed Bradley's First Army to expand to six corps of fifteen divisions. To ease the span of control of the American forces, General Eisenhower authorized General Bradley to form the 12th Army Group composed of the First Army on the left and the Third Army on the right of the line. On 1 August, the date set for the activation of 12th Army Group and Third Army, Generals Hodges and Patton assumed command of First Army and Third Army respectively. Patton's Third Army consisted of the XV Corps, the XX Corps, and the XII Corps.

Operation Cobra, the designated operation to break through at St. Lo, commenced with multiple air attacks, including carpet-bombing by heavy bombers to soften German resistance. The air attacks took place on 24 and 25 July inflicting heavy casualties on the German forces, as well as some American troops in forward positions. By the time General Patton took command of the newly activated Third Army, the VII Corps and the VIII Corps had broken through the German defenses and advanced as far south as Avaranches at the southern edge of the Cotentin peninsula.

Operation Overlord, the plan for the invasion of Normandy and the build up of the Allied forces, called for the early capture of the ports in the Brittany peninsula to augment the Allied logistic capability, which remained dependent upon re-supply over the initial beachheads secured on D-Day. Given the success of Operation Cobra and the rapid advance of the American forces to Avranches, opinions differed regarding the priorities stated in the Overlord plan, with General Montgomery advocating an alteration of the plan in favor of enveloping the German Seventh Army opposing the Allied invasion force.

General Bradley directed Patton to accomplish both tasks, liberating the Brittany ports while simultaneously pushing to the south and east to envelop the Germans. Patton directed the 4th and 6th Armored Divisions to drive to the west to secure the ports of Brest and St. Lorient respectively, while he wheeled the remainder of his three corps in a deep penetration securing Nantes and Angers to the south and then swung his XV Corps to the east and north to complete the encirclement of the German Seventh Army. The editors of the *Army Times* succinctly captured Patton's dynamic style of leadership: "The lesson Patton had imparted again and again throughout his career — that once you have the enemy reeling, you should never give him a moment's respite – had been learned with a vengeance. Gratified as he was, he insisted on still more shock action, more speed, more audacity."

General Patton captured Argentan on the eastern flank of the German Seventh Army and launched probing attacks to take Falaise, but his progress was halted by General Bradley who feared a collision with the Canadian First Army pushing down from the north with the mission of capturing Falaise. Regrettably, Montgomery's determination to avoid massive casualties – the British had lost nearly an entire generation during their offensive operations of World War I – resulted in an overly cautious attack that lacked sufficient force to overcome German resistance. The inadequately supported British attack failed to complete the double envelopment. As a result, a gap remained between the pincers of that envelopment, allowing German forces to escape the trap. General Montgomery's failure to fully support the operation delayed the encirclement of the German Seventh Army in what was to become known as the Falaise pocket.

Meanwhile, a major battle developed in the west when Hitler directed the German Seventh Army to attack to the sea to cut the Third Army supply lines through Avaranches. The First Army, under General Hodges, counterattacked to block the German assault halting the combined attacks of armored, airborne infantry and infantry divisions in a bitter fight at Mortain that inflicted heavy casualties on the enemy.

While these events unfolded, the German High Command began to show the strains of the war and bitterly fought campaign. Spitfire fighters caught Field Marshal Rommel's command car, destroying the vehicle and leaving him critically injured. Rommel was replaced by Field Marshal von Kluge, whose tenure in command was cut short as Hodges' First Army defeated the Germans at Mortain with heavy losses, especially from fighter-bomber attacks that left the roads littered with destroyed German vehicles, many of which were caught in snarled traffic and simply abandoned by their crews. Due to allied air attacks, von Kluge had to abandon his vehicle and remained out of communications with Hitler for twenty-four hours, a claim German authorities doubted because of an attempt on the life of the Fuhrer that had occurred in East Prussia. When ordered by Hitler to continue the unsuccessful attacks at Mortain to sever the Americans' supply lines in the west, von Kluge objected that the German Seventh Army was being encircled and had to commence an immediate withdrawal to the east. Hitler relieved von

Kluge and ordered him to report to his headquarters. Von Kluge never completed the trip as he took his own life by way of cyanide poisoning rather than face charges of conspiracy in the plot to kill the Fuhrer.

General Patton continued to pressure General Bradley for permission to close the gap in the Falaise pocket, but he was told to hold in place. Even with Third Army halted and enduring repeated attacks by German Panzer units attempting to break out of the encirclement, it held the southern shoulder of the envelopment. At the same time, Allied fighter bombers inflicted heavy losses on the German units attempting to escape through the fifteen-mile gap between Falaise and Argentan. The gap finally closed when Patton's troops made contact with elements of the Canadian First Army.

The Allies captured over 50,000 German prisoners in the trap. In addition, an estimated 10,000 Germans died in the pocket. The vehicle count of destroyed and captured vehicles included 220 tanks, 160 assault guns, 700 towed artillery pieces, 130 antiaircraft guns, 130 half tracks, 5,000 other motor vehicles, as well as 2,000 wagons and 1,800 dead horses. The Germans estimated that the units captured or destroyed in the encirclement constituted 50 percent of their Seventh Army. Despite the loss of life and equipment, most of the German high command survived the disaster. Of the fifteen German division commanders in the encirclement, all but three escaped. Of the five corps commanders in the encirclement, all but one escaped.

The rapid envelopment of the German Seventh Army by Patton's Third Army resulted in the first decisive defeat of the *Wehrmacht* in the West and shortened the war accordingly. General Patton's instinctive appreciation of the limitations of his opponents and his inspired leadership made the encirclement possible, despite General Montgomery's failure to seize his objective in a timely manner. Unfortunately, the capture of the entire German Seventh Army eluded the Allies as a result of the stalled attack to take Falaise.

Speaking to his staff following the operation, General Patton claimed, "The Third Army has advanced further and faster than any army in the history of the war." General Patton's rapid and deep encirclement of the German army west of the Seine was instrumental in securing the first major victory of the invasion forces in France. Throughout the remainder of the war, Patton repeatedly demonstrated his genius in major battles in which he outperformed his German opponents, while surpassing the performance of all other Allied commanders. He next demonstrated his brilliant leadership in the rapid liberation of central France as well as the Battle of the Bulge, where Third Army inflicted heavy punishment on the Germans in a massive counterattack, launched in record time, against the south flank of the penetration. General Patton again demonstrated his genius with his army's surprise assault river crossings of the Rhine River, despite the fact the majority of the Allied forces and logistics had been allocated to support Montgomery's assault river crossing of the Rhine in the north.[1] The Third Army's continued aggressive exploitation following the Rhine River crossing resulted in the occupation of vast areas of Germany and Czechoslovakia. No commander or army equaled the record established by General Patton and Third Army despite efforts by the British press and Field Marshal Montgomery to downplay General Patton's accomplishments and to take undeserved credit for the Allied victories.

[1] The major assault river crossing in the north was intended to hasten the capture of the launch sites of the V1 and V2 missiles that were inflicting heavy damage on targets in southern England at the time.

TWO
VIETNAM ADVISORY CAMPAIGNS

The Vietnam Advisory Campaigns grew out of containment, the strategy fashioned by the Truman and Eisenhower administrations to halt the spread of communism. The Marshal plan, NATO, and the Truman Doctrine blocked Soviet expansion in Europe, resulting in forward deployed American military forces in Europe as well as the formation of American strategic nuclear forces that provided a threat of retaliation in the event of Soviet attacks upon our forward deployed forces. Following the victory of the Chinese Communist Liberation Army in the Peoples' Republic of China (PRC), containment of communist expansion extended into Northeast Asia resulting in the Korean War, which brought a halt to the expansion of North Korean and Chinese Communist forces in the region after a bitter three years conflict. Following the termination of hostilities in Korea, containment faltered in Southeast Asia in the face of massive Chinese aid to the Viet Minh, which led to the collapse of the French colonial regime in Indochina in 1954 due, in part, to American reluctance to support French colonialism.

Following the separation of Vietnam at the 17th Parallel and France's withdrawal from its former colony, the Eisenhower Administration pledged to support the Geneva Accords that formally recognized the creation of a free and independent South Vietnam. American military and economic assistance was provided to

the Government of South Vietnam (GVN) in an effort to foster democratic
development in the region and protect against aggression from the North.

So it was that containment of communist aggression extended to Southeast Asia,
creating a barrier to Marxist-Leninist revolutionary warfare in the region and
posing a challenge to the Soviet Union and the PRC. Two weeks prior to the
inauguration of John F. Kennedy, Soviet Party Secretary Nikita Khrushchev made
a public announcement that the Soviet Union would support wars of national
liberation in undeveloped countries, which implied an effort to overleap the barrier
of containment. Khrushchev's announcement posed a direct challenge to the United
States and specifically to its newly elected president. Kennedy responded to the
challenge with the stirring words of his inaugural address, which pledged American
support to nations seeking to defend liberty in the face of renewed challenges of
communist aggression. These actions set the stage for the expanded American
advisory effort in South Vietnam, as well as for communist incursions from the
North to once again test American resolve.

– The Editors

Greater Love Hath No Man

The Story of Humbert Roque "Rocky" Versace
by Colonel James L. Abrahamson, USA (Ret.)

Initially held in a POW camp in Vietnam's Mekong Delta, Captain Rocky Versace encouraged and guided his fellow prisoners by inserting his own words into well-known songs, especially God Bless America, which he sang with gusto. Because of his influence with the other prisoners — and likely five months of his vehement criticism during the camp's political indoctrination sessions — the Viet Cong (VC) moved him to a smaller and more isolated facility. Long periods chained in a stifling six-foot by two-foot by three-foot elevated bamboo cage weakened him physically, as revealed by his last encounter with fellow-prisoner, Lieutenant Nick Rowe. At a nearby river, Rowe came upon Rocky in the act of washing his clothes — and characteristically arguing with his guard. From about two hundred yards away, Rowe called out encouragement to his friend. In a faint voice, Rocky replied: "Thank God you're here, Nick. God bless you."

After a brutal captivity only a month short of two years, the Viet Cong soon thereafter silenced by execution an American soldier whose spirit they could not break. Rowe later speculated that Rocky had "set an example as an American Officer that the Viet Cong could not tolerate having known to the world."

Captain Humbert R. Versace, 5th Special Forces Group, 1963.

While in high school, Rocky was torn between joining the priesthood or following his father to West Point and into the Army. Like his dad, he opted for the Military Academy, taking with him what his mother later described as his father's "fierce and demanding" love of country and a capacity to inspire and exhilarate others and make them feel secure. His West Point roommates recalled that the good-natured Rock "plugged away" and eventually "bulled his way through" every obstacle the academic and tactical departments put in his way. As an intramural wrestler and boxer — Brigade Open Wrestling Champion in his senior year — he developed his physical strength, agility, and capacity to withstand physical punishment. Fully embracing the Academy motto — Duty, Honor, Country — further strengthened a character already firmly grounded in his Roman Catholic faith.

Commissioned Armor, Rocky served with the 1st Cavalry Division in Korea before his assignment to Vietnam. Attached to the 5th Special Forces Group in Vietnam, he became S-2 advisor to the Vietnamese district chief in Ca Mau. A Marine, Don Price, who briefly served with Rocky, recalls that he was "incredibly strong for his size" and always carried a rosary and a pocket Bible. Though Price found him "close-mouthed and self-effacing," the Marine learned that the West Pointer he so admired liked most of all to talk about the Vietnamese, especially the children. Only later did Price learn that Rocky planned to enter the priesthood.

Despite the dangers of driving about Ca Mau district in a jeep while armed only with a pistol, Rocky kept in touch with the district orphanage, school, midwife facility, medical clinic, Catholic church, and a jail holding captured Viet Cong, whom he insisted be well treated. Except for an elderly priest, with whom Rocky chatted in French, he spoke with all in Vietnamese. Because he filled his pockets with hard candy, the children knew him as "Dai Uy Candy" — Captain Candy. Rocky Versace thus demonstrated the value of knowing the local languages and his great affection for the Vietnamese people and their culture. A model advisor, good natured and with a ready smile, Rocky impressed Price with his "subtle seriousness . . . . He was definitely a man on a mission."

About two weeks before the end of his tour in late 1963, when he had been released to proceed to Saigon for final clearance and administrative processing prior to his return to the States, a time most soldiers seek safe duty, Rocky returned for a last visit with his friends. While there, he volunteered to accompany two other Americans, Lieutenant Nick Rowe and Sergeant First Class Dan Pitzer, for an attack on a platoon-sized VC outpost. When the Viet Cong fled, the Vietnamese lieutenant ordered his company to pursue them — right into an ambush by a VC battalion. Even after receiving three bullet wounds to his leg, Rocky and the two other Americans covered their unit's withdrawal until the much larger enemy battalion overwhelmed and captured all three.

Rocky, having already demonstrated his dedication as an advisor, had now also shown great courage under fire as a troop leader protecting the lives of his men. The ordeal that eventually won him the Medal of Honor had only begun.

Often chained in a bamboo cage barely large enough to hold his tall frame, Rocky was vulnerable to nightly hordes of mosquitoes that blackened the surface of any bare skin. He was fed very little, received minimal medical attention, and endured regular interrogation sessions intended to elicit phony confessions of war crimes useful for Viet Cong propaganda purposes. Strictly adhering to the Code of Conduct, he gave his interrogators only the information required by the Geneva Conventions, from which he recited chapter and verse. Rocky's refusal to cooperate resulted in punishments that included beatings, confinement to a bamboo cage, and loss of the mosquito net essential for health in the remote region of the Mekong Delta where the prisoners were held.

During the political indoctrination, Rocky gave as good as he got — and more, often expressed in Vietnamese so that the guards as well as the political cadre could hear. By demanding that the Viet Cong treat his comrades well and making his resistance the center of the cadre's attention, he also took some of the pressure off his fellow prisoners. "You can make me come to this class," Nick Rowe recalled him telling the cadre, "but I am an officer in the United States Army. You can make me listen, and you can force me to sit here, but I don't believe a word of what you are saying, and frankly you can go to Hell!"

In the end, it was the Viet Cong who broke. Unable to make any headway with Rocky, frustrated with the way he inspired and looked out for the welfare of his fellow prisoners whenever not kept in solitary confinement, annoyed that despite his wounds he had made three unsuccessful attempts to escape, the cadre dealt with Rocky in a manner illustrative of their defeat. On 26 September 1965, after holding him prisoner for twenty-three months, the Viet Cong murdered Rocky Versace.

In a 1969 speech to cadets about his own captivity and ultimate escape after five years, Rowe said of Rocky: "This was a West Point graduate! I think the thing here is Rocky set an example. He died for what he believed in. He died for his actions, but he is a man who I believe will be remembered . . . . If anybody is in a situation similar, here is a man you can look up to . . . . He could have bent, he could have broken, he could have lived. But he chose not to because he was a West Pointer . . . . He was the greatest example of what an officer should be that I have ever come in contact with."

On 8 July 2002, while presenting to Rocky's brothers and sister the Medal of Honor—the first to be awarded to an Army POW for actions during captivity in Southeast Asia—President George W. Bush observed that Rocky had "traveled to a distant land to bring the hope of freedom to people he never met. In his defiance and later his death, he set an example of extraordinary dedication that changed the lives of his fellow soldiers who saw it firsthand. His story echoes across the years, reminding us of liberty's high price and of the noble passion that caused one good man to pay that price in full."[1]

[1] Though Captain Versace's remains have not been found, Arlington Cemetery contains his memorial tombstone a few yards from the graves of his parents.

Leadership by Example

by Colonel Andrew P. O'Meara, Jr., USA (Ret.)

In the early years of the War, American advisors assigned to Vietnamese army units as individuals soon became de facto members of the unit. We either spoke Vietnamese or made a valiant try to master the tonal language – a goal beyond the reach of those of us with a tin ear. We ate Vietnamese chow out of rice bowls with chopsticks. On combat operations, we slept on the ground beside our Vietnamese comrades. As our units received new equipment, we introduced the American weapons and tactics. When appropriate, we offered advice to our counterparts. When all else failed, we led by example, especially in combat when time was of the essence and words failed to bridge barriers to understanding.

I joined the Army of the Republic of Vietnam's 1st Cavalry Regiment in October 1962 as an Infantry Advisor to a mechanized infantry company equipped with newly fielded M-113s – the best armored personnel carrier on either side of the Iron Curtain. We operated across the length and breadth of the III Corps Tactical Zone, making forays into communist sanctuaries including War Zone D, War Zone C, and the Iron Triangle– the most dangerous Communist base in the Corps area and a thorn in our sides because it occupied terrain adjacent to Highway 13, the main supply route in the region. Our mechanized infantry companies consequently made multiple raids into the Iron Triangle to disrupt enemy operations.

Though we fought the Viet Cong, we were unable to destroy our enemy because a vast tunnel network that connected the enemy fighting positions greatly complicated clearing the Iron Triangle. The primary weapon of the enemy consisted of mine fields, covered by fire from well-concealed fighting positions connected by tunnels that permitted

Viet Cong snipers to inflict casualties on our units and withdraw unseen. There were twenty-seven kilometers of tunnels connecting the fortified hamlets of the Iron Triangle when we made our forays into the enemy base area, which meant that we never cleared more than a fraction of the enemy fortified zone during any one operation. Once the government troops withdrew, the Viet Cong re-occupied their base area and resumed their attacks on our convoys moving on Highway 13.

In the winter of 1963, I received word to accompany the Fourth Mechanized Infantry Company of the regiment on an extended

This picture shows Lieutenant O'Meara and Vietnamese friends of the First Cavalry Regiment with family members in February 1963 in the town of Dong Xoai. The regiment had one troop stationed as part of the garrison, which included Civil Guards. They treated me like a son or brother. Their friendship created a bond with Vietnamese comrades resisting communism that altered me forever. I had never experienced anything like their sincere friendship, and the experience created deep loyalties to the people of Vietnam.[1]

[1] The town was overrun by the North Vietnamese Army (NVA), which wiped out the entire garrison and the villagers. It was a Catholic village that had been resettled from the Red River Delta after the partition of Indochina. The Communists had an intense hatred of those who had fled the Communist North, which translated into a death sentence for those later captured by the VC or NVA. A Roman Catholic, I attended Mass with the villages during my stay in the village while awaiting the commencement of an operation into War Zone D. The media covered the fall of Dong Xoai, but they failed to fault the Communists for annihilating the villagers. They saved their criticism for the garrison that called in air strikes on their positions in a fruitless attempt to halt the Communist attacks.

operation in the Iron Triangle. Attached to an infantry battalion and supported by an engineer company for the assault on the Viet Cong base area, we planned to remain in the Iron Triangle for two months, digging out the tunnels and blowing up the underground complexes with the help of the engineers.

Commencing our initial assault, we encountered stiff resistance and took many casualties from mines and small arms fire. The infantry battalion and the engineers pushed down the main road from Ben Cat leading into the eastern sector of the enemy base area, clearing the Viet Cong's fortified positions in the process. Despite the enemy resistance, we pushed deep into the Iron Triangle. The mechanized infantry paralleled the progress of the dismounted infantry and engineers, covering their flank along the secondary jungle that covered the interior of the base area. We could hear the heavy explosions of the mines that punctuated the firefights as the enemy was driven deeper into his base area.

About mid-morning we got word that the engineer advisor, Captain Kenworthy, had been severely injured by a mine. The report made clear he would not survive without medical assistance. The task force halted and made attempts to reach Kenworthy, who was well forward in the midst of a heavily mined area that the engineers had been trying to clear. From the sounds of the explosions, we roughly pinpointed the location of the wounded advisor. I told my counterpart, Captain Thoan, that I would go to the aid of the stricken advisor. Captain Thoan told me, "Don't go O'Meara. It is a very dangerous area." I knew that to hesitate meant the loss of a brave comrade and told Thoan I had to try to save the man. I asked for volunteers to help me carry the advisor out of the mined area. The men looked at me with wide eyes, but none stepped forward.

Grabbing my M1 rifle, I dismounted from the track and with my heart in my throat, I began making my way toward the location of the officer. I watched carefully for mines, placing each foot on ground that was either well worn or marked with M113 tracks where our vehicles had traversed the area and either detonated the mines or severed their trip wires. I thus pushed forward in the direction of the firefight, using the narrow paths made by the tracks of the armored vehicles.

After moving forward carefully for what seemed an eternity, I spotted a Vietnamese medic kneeling over the wounded advisor. I quickly observed that Kenworthy had taken the full blast of the mine. He was unconscious, lying in a large puddle of dark blood, with multiple fragments in the face. His lower leg was nearly severed, and he had taken one piece of shrapnel through the left hand. The medic was bandaging his hand, a simple wound that the young Vietnamese medic felt he could handle. The life-threatening wound was the leg injury, which bled profusely. I removed my bootlaces to place a tourniquet above the knee. Then I took bandages from the medic's kit and heavily bandaged the lower leg.

With the bleeding stopped, I looked around for help because Kenworthy was too big for me to carry. The medic, not about to move deeper into the minefield, refused to help. I would have to return to Captain Thoan's command track to locate a stretcher and someone to help me carry the unconscious man out of the mined area. I gingerly made my way back through the minefield, placing my feet in footprints I had made when I entered the area. I found the command track and told Thoan I thought we could save the American advisor, but I would need a litter and someone to help me carry the unconscious man. I asked for volunteers from the unit. Again there were no takers.

I turned to an American staff officer from Saigon, who had asked to accompany the unit to observe our operation. I told him I now needed his help. Reluctant to go, he reminded me that the commander had strongly advised us not to enter the minefield. I told him: "If you don't come now, Kenworthy will die." He agreed to help. I grabbed a litter and told him to follow me, placing his feet where I placed mine. We carefully made our way back to Kenworthy's location. We placed him on the litter and began the difficult trek back through the danger area with the heavily laden litter. I led the way by placing my feet in the footprints I had previously made. After a difficult struggle along the circuitous route, we cleared the minefield and loaded the litter into the M113.

Captain Thoan requested a medical evacuation helicopter. Accompanied by a platoon of infantry, he then led the way down to open ground composed of rice paddies lined with paddy dikes. The dike running along the south side of the rice fields was a large one that bordered a canal. I told Thoan we would land the chopper on the south paddy dike, which was large enough to land a chopper. Again, comrades warned me not to venture out onto the paddy dike, which could have been mined to restrict movement into the area. We ignored the warnings. The staff officer and I dismounted the track with the litter and made our way out to the center of the dike, which had no obstructions that would hinder the landing of the chopper.

Presently we heard the *thump, thump, thump* of the chopper blades, and I saw the silhouette of the bird above the tree line. I threw a smoke grenade and guided the pilot to a safe landing. The crew chief dismounted, and I told him not to remove the tourniquet because Kenworthy had lost too much blood. He acknowledged my warning, and the crew of the medical evacuation chopper loaded the litter into the helicopter, which quickly lifted off.

The next day we got word from the American hospital in Saigon that the tourniquet had saved Kenworthy's life. Our efforts were not in vain. We saved a life and set an example that spoke more eloquently than mere words, demonstrating the importance of taking risks to save a comrade. Leadership by example had shown young soldiers the importance of immediate action to aid a comrade even when the situation looked hopeless. Prior to my departure from Vietnam, the Army recognized my actions to save a fellow advisor by the award of the Bronze Star for Valor.

Treachery
by Colonel Andrew P. O'Meara, Jr., USA (Ret.)

In the summer of 1963, a time of riots and demonstrations in Vietnam, the Buddhists were up in arms, and rumors of treason were daily fare in the foreign media. As I emerged from a barbershop in Saigon, clusters of illiterate dockworkers marched through the streets carrying signs written in English denouncing their government. Shoppers and merchants ignored the gaggle of demonstrators blocking traffic in the middle of Freedom Boulevard, which once bisected Saigon. American journalists ran along the cluster of ill-clad workers attempting to get enough bodies in their camera lenses to provide photographic evidence for stories that would appear in the *New York Times* proclaiming a demonstration of tens of thousands denouncing the "corrupt" Diem regime.

While drinking my morning coffee over the next few days, I read the newspaper accounts of the massive demonstration, realizing that I had seen no more than fifty workers obviously paid to carry signs they could not read. They could have been Viet Cong peasants, but their clothing suggested otherwise. Their absence from the docks was evidently rewarded in cash by enemies of Diem's government, encouraged by the attention of the foreign journalists. The result was a fabricated news event manufactured by coup plotters intent upon bringing down President Diem.

At the time, I was an American advisor who had spent the past year with South Vietnamese mechanized infantry units garrisoned near the city. Rumors of an imminent coup had circulated in the American press for some time. The reports of coup plotters served as a damper on our military operations as troops loyal to the president were recalled to their garrisons to ward off nebulous threats circulated by the journalists. As a result, my infantry comrades were restricted to their barracks, leaving me out of a job, while they occupied themselves cleaning weapons they had cleaned the day before.

My morning coffee was cut short by a call from my boss informing me that I had been reassigned as the advisor to the tank company commanded by Captain Ngai. A true professional needing no advisor, Ngai had commanded the company for five years. His primary duty was to furnish platoons of M24 light tanks to the Presidential Guard protecting the Palace.

Shortly after reporting to Captain Ngai, we received a mission as a rapid reaction force providing assistance to a strategic hamlet that had been overrun in Long Khan Province. Prior to our departure, my American boss told me to get the company's radio frequencies. I suggested he get the information from the unit's communications officer. He curtly replied that "we" don't want them to know that we are monitoring their radio frequencies. I realized instantly that I had become a plant in the ranks of the Presidential Guard – a spy posing as a battle-tested comrade and friend. The realization that I was being used to betray my comrades turned my stomach. I was being asked to betray soldiers I had lived with and fought beside over the previous year.

It was a long dusty ride before the belated reaction force made its appearance at the site of the strategic hamlet, whose residents were still cleaning up and burying the dead. We inspected the damage and spoke to the survivors. That evening Ngai and I took our meal together on a grass mat in a clearing that served as the tank company's night defensive position. Our meal consisted of rice and chicken, a luxury prepared by

47

Ngai's driver, who was a fine cook. We drank tea together after the meal and watched the sun set over the jungle canopy. As we shared our meal, I knew my personal honor and sense of duty as a trusted advisor and comrade-in-arms would not permit me to betray my friends.

Asked for the radio frequencies upon my return to the cavalry regiment's headquarters, I replied that I did not have them. I responded

First Lieutenant Andrew P. O'Meara, Jr., Military Assistance Command-Vietnam, 1963.

that it was not possible for me to record the radio frequencies, a response that made clear that I would not cooperate with coup planners in the CIA – or whoever was behind efforts to bring down President Diem.

My tour of duty in Vietnam nearly over, there was no work for me as an infantry advisor on combat operations that had come to a halt. Not working out in my newly assigned role as a spy, in a few days I received orders assigning me to stateside duty.

Within a few days of my arrival at my new duty station, Fort Knox, I read of the coup that took the life of President Diem. Scanning the newsstand to find information on the fate of my friends, my eyes fell upon the cover of *Life Magazine*. There on the cover was an armored personnel carrier of the Cavalry Regiment carrying the coffin of the leader of the coup attack. Prominently displayed on the front of the coffin was a picture of Captain Ngai. My eyes filled with tears as I struggled to control my emotions. A Vietnamese friend, Captain Tom, a member of the regiment attending the Armor School, told me the story of the coup.

Deceived into playing a leading role in the coup, Captain Ngai had been told that coup forces were approaching the Palace and ordered to take his tank company to reinforce the Presidential Guard. He took his company down the middle of Freedom Boulevard, riding in the lead tank as was his custom. As his tank company approached the Palace, an M8 armored car of the Palace Guard took him under fire. Its 37-mm armor-piercing round hit the turret of Ngai's light tank, penetrating the armor plate, striking him in the hips, and removing his legs at the waist. Using his arms to support his weight in the turret, he made his final radio transmission: "This is Six. Take all your commands from Five. Out." Then he fell down onto the turret floor and bled to death.

Ngai's actions are a priceless example of bold leadership and self-sacrifice under fire. Already knowing he was a dead man, Ngai did his duty. With all the strength that remained in his mortally wounded body, he passed his command to his executive officer. It was a brave act of a brave man, whose only thought was for his men and their difficult mission despite wounds that had literally torn him apart. Faithful to the last, Ngai did his duty. After the capture of the Palace, Ngai's soldiers wept when they learned of the fate of their brave commander. I am proud to this day to have served with that courageous soldier, whose example inspired his men and those of us fortunate to count him as our friend.

THREE
AMERICAN MILITARY
CAMPAIGNS *in* VIETNAM

The war in Vietnam changed character following the assassination of President John F. Kennedy. It happened gradually in response to an increase in the number of North Vietnamese (NVA) troop units sent south by Hanoi to carry out attacks upon American advisors, their support troops, and bases in South Vietnam. American combat forces were introduced into the war to protect the air bases and advisory compounds that had become the target of well-planned and aggressively executed attacks that took a heavy toll on American lives and equipment. Hanoi then stepped up its support of the war in the south in response to the introduction of American combat forces protecting the American advisory campaign. The escalation of enemy invaders from the North caused a fateful change that saw the introduction of American troop units in force to hunt down and destroy the communist ground forces that had fundamentally altered the war. The American strategy became a series of battles launched to halt the invasion from the North. Major NVA units, officially designated the Peoples' Army of Vietnam (PAVN), soon engaged in hard-fought battles with American troop units. The following leadership vignettes have as their background American combat operations in South Vietnam, U.S. Air Force missions flown in support of ground combat operations, and measures taken by the American anti-war movement to curtail support for the war on the home front, to include impeding recruitment of ROTC candidates on college campuses.
— The Editors

51

Leadership along the "Street Without Joy"

by Major General Nicholas Krawciw, USA (Ret.)

Responding to the Tet Offensive of 1968, II Field Force ordered the 3rd Squadron of the 5th Cavalry, part of the 9th Infantry Division, to the I Corps Tactical Zone. The squadron moved by sea from Bear-Cat, near Saigon, some 500 miles north to a beachhead known as Wunder Beach, named in honor of a Marine Corps colonel. A year earlier, elements of the 3rd Marine Division had landed there before moving further north to Quang-Tri province abutting the demilitarized zone dividing Vietnam. Wunder Beach lay a few miles from an old dirt road that ran between Quang-Tri city and Hue, the ancient capital of Vietnam. Writing in the Fifties about the French experience in Indochina, Bernard Fall entitled his book *Street Without Joy* for the many bitter battles that had occurred there. The book became one of the most popular accounts of the war between the French and the Vietminh. Accompanying U. S. Marines near the road in 1967, while engaged in writing a sequel to his earlier book, Bernard Fall was killed by a land mine.

Prior to my return for a second tour of duty in Vietnam, I studied Fall's book and had a copy with me as I joined the 3rd Squadron in July 1968. As operations officer, I helped the squadron commander plan and execute the unit's activities in our area of operations (AO), which included the infamous "Street." During that time, the squadron served under the operational control of the 3rd Brigade, 1st Cavalry Division. The 1st Cavalry was engaged in operations that sought to cut off NVA units that had infested Hue during the Tet Offensive in February and March 1968. By July 1968, with most of the NVA units defeated, their scattered remnants tried to work their way back to North Vietnam.

A week or two after my arrival, scouts of one of our cavalry troops located remnants of two NVA battalions retreating from Hue toward one of the villages in our AO. The 1st Cavalry division placed the 1st and 2nd Squadrons, 5th Cavalry under 3rd Brigade control in a historic reconstitution of the 5th Cavalry Regiment. The brigade quickly surrounded and decimated the NVA forces by piling on with the fires of attack helicopters, artillery, and the vehicle mounted machine guns of tanks and ACAVs (M113 personnel carriers with three machine guns behind shields on each vehicle). Some of our M48 tanks fired flachette anti-personnel rounds at the surrounded enemy troops, inflicting many casualties.

Following this battle, the squadron continued to search for other NVA and VC remnants in the villages along the "Street" and in the piedmont of hills west of Highway 1, the main north-south artery of Vietnam. The squadron searched for NVA stay-behind cadres and for local VC guerrillas who had survived the American counter-offensive after Tet. Soon the pace of operations slowed, old timers left for new assignments, and many new troopers arrived daily. In the fall of 1968, Lieutenant Colonel Thomas Carpenter III, USMA Class of 1958, joined us as the new squadron commander. I was thrilled because he was an old friend and a fellow soccer player at West Point under Coach Joe Palone. In 1968, as he entered his tenth year of service, the Army promoted my friend to lieutenant colonel (LTC) ahead of his peers and selected him to command the 3rd Squadron.

Shortly after assuming command, Carpenter began to train and coach the unit to improve the professionalism of both old and new troopers. After more than a year in Vietnam, the squadron had lost most of its old-timers. Fortunately, a few key noncommissioned officers extended, and we gained some good new ones, including a great officer, Sergeant Major (SGM) Love. Because most of the new troop commanders and platoon leaders lacked combat and leadership experience, LTC Carpenter reinstituted intensive unit and individual training, most of it done while the squadron conducted day and night search and clear missions. He demanded that leaders use proper "troop leading procedures" for every type of combat mission and that they not neglect maintenance of weapons and equipment.

At the same time, unlike the previous commander who stayed in the background, Tom led "from the front." We had two OH-6 observation helicopters, called loaches by the aviators, piloted by First Lieutenant Dunn and Warrant Officer Maxwell. During daylight hours, either Colonel Carpenter or I were in the air in one of the loaches to observe activities of units conducting the searches, scout ahead of them, or control fires and reinforcements during engagements. Sometimes both of us were in the air covering different parts of our AO.

During one of these search and clear operations in November of 1968, LTC Carpenter exhibited the character and leadership that were his exemplary traits throughout his career. It happened shortly after the 1st Cavalry Division moved to another area of South Vietnam, and the 101st Airborne Division (Airmobile) assumed operational control of the 3rd Squadron. Like the 1st Cavalry Division, the 101st habitually reinforced the squadron with one or two infantry companies. We would reorganize our cavalry troops and the infantry companies to form cavalry-infantry teams and assign each team an area to search and clear. Normally, the team commanders had the infantry searching the thickets in and around villages

Major Nick Krawciw (left) with Lt. Col. Tom Carpenter in Bu-Long Valley in Spring 1969.

while the cavalry platoons provided over watch or moved along with the infantry in less dense terrain.

Following their defeat during and after Tet, the surviving VC holed up in many of the villages west of the "Street" hiding in the underground bunkers and tunnels within its war-torn villages. Mines and booby traps became their main defenses. As a result, our attached infantry and ACAVs suffered daily casualties.

Prior to this operation, one platoon of a rifle company working with us had suffered seven booby-trap casualties in three consecutive days. As the search progressed on the fourth day, this rifle platoon was approaching a village when a booby-trapped howitzer round exploded and tore apart a young sergeant, a well-liked and respected leader, and wounded two other soldiers. Both the squadron commander and I were in the air. He was over the area of the explosion and called me to the scene. Landing, I saw that medics were doing their best to save the young sergeant as well as treat the other wounded. The squadron commander, meanwhile, tried to calm the remaining members of the rifle platoon. Some were crying and others chambered rounds into their weapons announcing their intention to go through the village shooting everyone in the belief that the villagers were responsible for the booby traps. Only a few NCOs seemed to have control of their emotions.

Tom had the entire platoon, including the distraught platoon leader, sit down, cool it, and disassemble their weapons for cleaning. He told me he would stay with the platoon to ensure it did not do something dumb. He wanted me to evacuate the sergeant, who had lost both legs and an arm, to the hospital ship near our AO in the South China Sea. The medics placed the badly wounded sergeant on the back seats of the OH-6, and Warrant Officer Maxwell and I flew him to the hospital ship. In fifteen minutes, we landed on its deck and placed the young man under the care of doctors and nurses. Medevac helicopters picked up the other wounded.

When I think back to that day, I remain convinced that LTC Carpenter prevented another My-Lai. At that time (1968), we had not heard about the My-Lai massacre. When disclosed a year or two later, the incident became the cause of great shame for the Army and its leaders for failure to prevent a massacre of old men, women, and children.

Carpenter remained in command of the 3rd Squadron, 5th Cavalry through 1968 into the spring and summer of 1969. The training he instituted paid off when in February 1969 the squadron, while under the control of Colonel Jim Gibson's 1st Brigade, 5th Infantry Division (Mechanized), repelled coordinated attacks by the 27th and 33rd NVA regiments. During this heavy fighting, the squadron established its base at Con-Thien, a key outpost that was part of "Leatherneck Square" in the 3rd Marine Division's AO. At the end of the battles in that area, Colonel Gibson told Colonel Carpenter that a message from the 27th NVA Regiment's commander had been intercepted, requesting permission from Hanoi to return to North Vietnam, suggesting the unit had taken heavy casualties.

Later, in May, June, and July of 1969, LTC Carpenter led the Squadron with minimal losses into the Ashau Valley in support of the 3rd Brigade of the 101st Division, commanded by Colonel Joe B. Conmy, Class of '43. The Squadron's presence in the valley may have been what triggered the NVA to reinforce with large units and eventually precipitate the "Hamburger Hill" battle.

I remember Tom Carpenter's leadership and courage under fire in all these operations. Of the challenges he faced, the most memorable was his action along the "Street Without Joy," where his leadership calmed hurt and excited soldiers. Leading from the front in a difficult and emotionally charged situation, he saved our Army from what could have been another terrible and shameful incident.

25 August 1966

by Brigadier Gerneral William J. Mullen III, USA (Ret.)

First Infantry Division headquarters named it the Battle of Bong Trang, but the American soldiers who made war there always called it 25 August. That's the day in 1966 when my unit fought the Phu Loi Battalion, a Viet Cong main force unit, in its fortified camp twenty-five miles north of Saigon.

The firefight started when an ambush patrol from Charlie Company, 1st Battalion, 2d Infantry, walked into the VC position during breakfast.

Brigadier General William J. Mullen III, USA (Ret.).

The fight got bigger when the rest of C Company, riding with a platoon from Charlie Troop, 1st Squadron, 4th Cavalry, crashed into the fortified VC base camp in an effort to reach the patrol. The fight got bigger yet as companies from the 1st Battalion, 2d Infantry, 1st Battalion, 26th Infantry, 1st Battalion, 16th Infantry, and 2d Battalion, 28th Infantry reinforced the contact.

An initially minor skirmish quickly grew into a brutal all-day fight at close quarters in thick vegetation with a tough enemy who was dug in with automatic weapons, some of which were heavy. We had an edge with the 1-5 Artillery and the Air Force, which provided continuous supporting fire and air strikes. The outcome, though, came down to the hard fighting of the soldiers on the ground. We were trying to evict the VC from their holes; they wanted to stay. Colonel Sid Berry, First Brigade Commander, called the battle the most intense firefight he had seen in Korea or Viet Nam. The casualties show the viciousness of the battle. The Big Red One, as the 1st Infantry Division was known, lost 30 killed and 183 wounded, many of them officers and NCOs. Based on captured documents, the VC lost 171 combatants killed in action; their wounded filled all their medical facilities in the region.

Early the next morning, the patrol's survivors linked up with us. From all accounts there were many heroic actions among all the units involved. I witnessed some of them. They are as vivid today as they were then.

Specialist Ira Turpin, with a quick joke and a few men, charged down a trench line to clear it and defend part of our position.

Throughout the heavy fighting, our medics displayed their quiet competence and bravery.

Until Second Lieutenant Bruce Robertson, our forward observer, was evacuated, he called for artillery fires on a continuous basis, despite blood spurting from multiple wounds.

Captain Jim Madden, commanding B Company of the 26th Infantry, one of the first units to fight its way into our location, received a serious wound almost as soon as he reached us. He nevertheless broke away from the medics in order to apologize to me for having to leave the fight.

Private First Class Dennis Peterson, a member of the ambush patrol, provided leadership and first aid to his wounded comrades all day and through the night before leading the survivors to safety. In the course of the fighting, Sergeant Gene Glasscock, the artillery reconnaissance sergeant with the ambush patrol, repulsed VC attacks by calling fire on his own position.

An indelible memory for me is that of Captain Pete Knight, A Company of the 1st Battalion, 16th Infantry. Upon entering our position, he immediately assured me everything was going to be all right. He was killed moments later as he led his men in an assault on an entrenched VC position.

My most enduring memory, though, is of one of Charlie Company's mortar-men. While talking on the radio, I heard someone say, "Charlie Six." I looked up to see Specialist Tommy Freese, the only man in his platoon not a casualty. As bullets flew all around, Tommy stood in the open with a 60-mm mortar on one shoulder and a sack of ammunition on the other. "Sir," he said, "the Fourth Platoon is ready. Where do you want me to shoot?"

On 25 August each of these men did his very best. That willingness, under conditions of violent and mortal danger, has been the hallmark of American soldiers since the Revolutionary War. Officers and noncommissioned officers have to master the tools of their trade in order to be their very best when called upon to lead such soldiers in battle where violence and mortal danger complicate decision making.

Leadership under Fire

by Major General John S. Grinalds, USMC (Ret.)

The following story about leadership is inspired by my experience as a Marine officer in Vietnam. It is a story about a twenty-year-old Marine enlisted man, Lance Corporal Alfred J. Herring, whose actions exemplified for me what constitutes leadership under duress. The memory of his actions constantly reminds me that service to others is the essence of leadership.

Herring, from Mullins, South Carolina, was the only boy in his high school class to go to Vietnam. He enlisted in the Marine Corps after graduation and was soon serving in H Company, 2nd Battalion, 1st Marines. I was the S-3 of the battalion on 20 September 1970 when

Herring and his patrol left their company position near Danang to set up an ambush nearby. Viet Cong rocket teams would try to approach the Danang Air Base and shell the field at night. The mission of Herring's patrol was, along with the many other patrols out each night, to interdict the approach of Viet Cong rocket teams.

That night, Herring's patrol leader set up the Marines in a tight circle around a trail junction. Each rifleman covered an approaching trail like the spokes of a wheel. The patrol leader, the corpsman, and Herring, the radioman, moved to the center of the ambush site.

What they didn't know was a booby trap was already there – an 81-mm mortar round on a stake rigged with a tripwire. The patrol leader set it off, killing him and the corpsman instantly. Herring, outboard of the blast, was bowled over but came to his senses in a moment. Enemy fire poured into the position. Herring returned fire intermittently as he crawled around the position to check on his buddies. Everyone was incapacitated, either dead or seriously wounded.

The battalion operations center heard Herring come up on his company net, "Hotel, this is Hotel One Alpha. We have KIA and WIA. Request medevac and covering fires." Over the next thirty minutes a remarkable saga evolved.

As the two CH-46 medevac helicopters approached his position from the north, Herring shifted the artillery to the south and brought the birds under the rounds' trajectory and into the trail junction, door guns blazing. Then he and a crew chief went around the position moving the dead and wounded aboard the helicopters under the door guns' covering fire. Each time they brought one of his buddies aboard, Herring would radio their status. His last call was, "Hotel, this is One Alpha. All KIA and WIA aboard. Departing LZ. Request covering fires on LZ. Out."

The helicopters exited to the north and the artillery clobbered the ambush area. The helicopters went over our operations center a few minutes later en route to the field hospital. We began making inquiry of the hospital about the casualties and their condition. We were stunned to learn that Herring had died. He had been wounded during the action and bled to death. Little did we know that his last words over the net were his last words on earth. Even as he checked out of the net with his last word, "Out," he was checking out of this mortal life.

Eventually, an award recommendation was submitted but then lost amidst the confusion of combat operations. Years later, his buddies, whose lives he had saved, resurrected the case, and in late 1996, Herring's mother was presented his Navy Cross at Marine Corps Recruit Depot, Parris Island, SC.

I have had over thirty years to think about what Lance Corporal Herring did in the last hour of his life. His actions exhibited all the leadership qualities we hope to see in our young combat leaders. First of all, he knew his stuff. He was professionally competent. He knew his radio. He could handle his weapon. He was effective at the complicated process of coordinating artillery fires and a medevac extraction under fire. He also knew first aid and how to deal with traumatic wounds.

Herring was also courageous. He could have just hugged the earth and waited for the cavalry to arrive. Instead, he moved around the ambush site, exposing himself to enemy fire, tending to his buddies, and risking the worst. He risked, also, the possibility of failure at this responsibility thrust upon him. Herring was, for the moment, the only man who could act and he bravely stepped into the huge gap between his rank and experience and what needed to be done.

In addition, Herring was entirely selfless. As he crawled around the perimeter caring for the wounded, he made decision after decision in favor of them. He used his compress bandages on them, and he used his belt and even his bootlaces as tourniquets. All the while his own lifeblood was pouring out. If he had tended first to himself, he might be alive today. Rather, like Jesus Christ, he poured himself out for others. "Greater love hath no man than that he lay down his life for his fellow man."

Lance Corporal Alfred J. Herring, 1st Marines, 1970.

Duty, Honor, Country. Lance Corporal Alfred J. Herring's actions in the last hour of his life best exemplify to me the meaning of our alma mater's motto. God bless his memory and West Point's efforts to prepare its graduates to meet similar challenges.

Unsung Victories of American Airmen

by Colonel Andrew P. O'Meara, Jr., USA (Ret.)

I returned to South Vietnam in 1968, joining the 11th Armored Cavalry Regiment operating north of Saigon under the operational control of the 1st Infantry Division. I found myself taking part in a hard fought series of battles as we sought to destroy enemy base camps established in the jungles south of War Zone D. These camps formed fortified staging areas constructed along multiple parallel routes to the south that permitted the enemy to move combat forces out of Cambodia from one protected battle position to the next in their invasion of South Vietnam. More significantly, the base camps acted as fortified assembly areas for staging NVA attacks upon American air bases and logistical support units located north of Saigon.

The battlefield the enemy had selected to contest covered jungle terrain that suited the short-range weaponry that the NVA brought to the conflict in the early years of the struggle, when Hanoi maintained the war of the National Liberation Front (NLF) was an indigenous insurgency.[1] The jungle restricted visibility to a few yards as American infantrymen and cavalrymen searched for their opponents, and it negated the superiority of the long-range weapons and technology the Americans brought to the battle.

The enemy's base camps consisted of bunkers with overhead cover and extensive trench lines. The troops were armed with Soviet assault rifles and machine guns. Chinese Claymore-type mines covering the approaches to fortifications augmented deadly short-range weapons. Situated beneath dense jungle canopy often two hundred feet in height, the enemy was protected from aerial observation, artillery fire which detonated prematurely in the tall canopy of the rain forests, and the ground incursions required to overwhelm the enemy's positions one trench and one bunker at a time. We were winning the battles, for at the end of the day we owned the enemy base camp that had been the target of our attacks. Even so, the grim statistics of the battles yielded no joy.

With our dead and wounded often as numerous as those of our enemy, we engaged in an exhausting form of battle that sapped the strength of our soldiers in the heat of the tropical rain forests. The fighting also tested the tactical skills of our troops, who learned to approach the enemy bunkers from the blind side and grenade the occupants, allowing small teams of expert infantry to move through a large bunker complex and inflict heavy casualties on our opponents. Even so, victory did not come cheap. The deadly game of seeking

[1] Later in the war, following the decimation of the Viet Cong military formations and the elimination of the Viet Cong infrastructure by the Phoenix Program, the NVA employed conventional tactics using divisional size units fully equipped with Soviet heavy equipment including tanks and artillery. By 1972 the NLF insurgency had failed and all pretext of NLF control of the North's war effort in South Vietnam was abandoned, despite the fact that the NLF continued to play a role in the Paris Peace Talks as a diplomatic ploy to bring about a settlement based upon communist participation in the government of South Vietnam (GVN).

Aero Rifle Platoon members (ARPs) posing with captured enemy weapons after successfully clearing an enemy bunker complex, a dangerous and often costly operation. The individuals from left to right are Sergeant Butler, Sergeant Roeder, Lieutenant Doubleday, Specialist Starkey, and Sergeant Summers.

out the enemy's fortified positions proved costly as American troops encountered the well-concealed mines and snipers of the enemy. Once locked in battle, the set piece slaughter began as the American infantry and cavalry troopers took out the enemy, one bunker at a time.

Bitter, exhausting, and costly engagements characterized the battles for the enemy base camps. My boss, Colonel George S. Patton III, a resolute fighter, commanded the 11th Armored Cavalry Regiment. Colonel Patton took care of his men, and his troopers worshiped him in return. We were vexed by the complexity of the problem of reducing the well-constructed base camps of our tenacious opponents. Assigned as the S-2 (intelligence officer) of the regiment, I had been watching reports of the battles being waged to destroy the enemy headquarters and base camps along the Cambodian border. These battles had a different character, which pitted the skills of the American air cavalry and the firepower of Air Force B52 strikes to obliterate the enemy. The jungle canopy offered no protection to the massive bomb strikes that literally blew away the massive hardwood trees that grew to great heights. I realized that the battles on the Cambodian frontier made much better use of the American advantages in technology and firepower than our bloody approach to the problem.

I asked Colonel Patton if he would authorize the request of Air Force B52 strikes to destroy the enemy's prepared battle positions in our AO. He challenged me saying: "Do you have the intelligence to justify that expenditure of firepower?" I swallowed hard and answered yes. I had confidence in our intelligence analysis section headed up by Captain Ralph Rosenberg and in our intelligence collection capabilities, especially the scouts of the regiment's Air Cavalry Troop. Patton thought about my proposal and responded that if the intelligence section could produce the data to justify an "Arc Light Strike," the code name given to B52 strikes, he would support the request.

I took the problem to the commander of the Air Cavalry Troop, Major John C. Bahnsen, who immediately recognized the advantages of fighting from our strengths, rather than allowing the enemy to dictate the terms of battle. He was a great fighter and a smart tactician who recognized that the search for the enemy base camps called for close coordination between the scouts and those of us in the regimental intelligence section engaged in working up the request for B52 strikes. He promptly gave me direct access to his scouts, telling them that they would be working directly for the S-2 in developing B52 targets until they were needed to destroy a communist unit brought to bay in the open terrain that formed the western portion of 11th Cavalry area of operations. He added that our Arc Light targeting effort was too important and the time too precious to waste on intermediary links in the chain of reporting.

I fashioned specific AOs for each of our eight scout teams. These teams were referred to as pink teams and were composed of one light observation helicopter and one cobra gunship providing cover and communication links to the operations section of the troop. I took the scout teams out one by one and showed them the limits of their assigned area. I also showed them the enemy trails identified from previous scout reports, intelligence carefully collated and preserved by Ralph Rosenberg and the men working for him. The scouts intuitively recognized the advantages of the new method of attacking the enemy. They did not need to be told that many American soldiers would no longer leave Viet Nam in body bags if we could locate the base camps from the air and bring down on our enemy massive fire from the sky. In the days and weeks that followed, the scouts of the Air Cavalry Troop identified multiple enemy base camps in the jungle. We took the intelligence to the 1st Infantry Division and II Field Force, where we convinced our superiors of the lucrative targets that were providing sanctuaries to enemy troop units preparing to launch attacks upon American installations at Bien Hoa and Long Binh. The Arc Light Strikes were approved.

Most of our B52 strikes went in during the night or at first light. Colonel Patton directed his operations officer, Lieutentant Colonel Jim Dozier, to follow up B52 strikes with ground troops. I worked with the scouts to prepare the Bomb Damage Assessments (BDA) of the strikes. The Arc Light strikes had produced awesome results, obliterating base camps, blasting away the tall jungle canopy, and bringing down trees that once obscured observation. Huge craters plowed the ground that formerly housed formidable communist combat units and logistical support troops. Cadavers hung out of the trees on the perimeter of the strike zone. Only splinters remained of massive trees, and the muck and dirt thrown skyward during the bomb blasts now covered the ground in a carpeted layer several feet thick that obscured human body parts dismembered in the attack. Regrettably, the earth did not conceal the stench of human guts and brains that now saturated the carpet of newly plowed ground, formerly the site of extensive trenches and bunker complexes.

We were elated but hard pressed to describe the results of the BDA. We could count the cadavers hanging from the trees, but we had no idea of the numbers of enemy soldiers incinerated by the blasts. Nor could we imagine the number of NVA survivors who fled toward the Cambodian border as fast as they could to evade our post-strike reconnaissance operations. We did not learn of the massive losses we had inflicted upon the enemy until weeks later, when captured prisoners revealed during interrogation that they had been members of a unit stationed in one of the enemy base camps targeted for attack by the B52s. Whole companies and battalions had virtually ceased to exist in the succession of massive explosions that had obliterated the communist base camps. By then it was difficult to claim the enemy casualties inflicted in a battle that had taken place weeks, if not months, before. The skeptical journalists denied our claims. They claimed we were lying to make our commanders look good. They were wrong.

As hoped, the use of Arc Light Strikes in the fight of the 11th Armored Cavalry Regiment against NVA base camps dramatically reduced our casualties. The large number of body bags headed to Long Binh on their way to grieving family members of the 11th Cavalry troopers fell sharply. The aircrews of the B52s flying at 25,000 feet could see nothing of their targets except jungle canopy. They had no way of knowing the impact their long and exhausting missions had on our combat operations, especially in view of the fact that the media, reflecting Hanoi's propaganda, derided the value of the strikes. But we knew and were grateful.

I am confident that I would not have survived my tour of duty with the 11th Cavalry had it not been for the men of the Air Force, who saved the lives of infantrymen and cavalry troopers by sparing them bitter battles to demolish enemy base camps. Words cannot convey our gratitude to the brave Air Force leaders and crewmen who made possible our victories and saved the lives of countless American fighting men.

Mentoring Responsible Leaders

by Lieutenant Colonel Nathaniel F. Colby, USA (Ret.)

Trust between commanders is the foundation of successful leadership. While acting as coach and mentor, senior officers must allow subordinate commanders to err and learn without severe penalty. The absence of trust is not necessarily an adverse reflection on the subordinate, but it may reflect the senior commander's lack of confidence in his or her abilities. With very few exceptions, those appointed to command a platoon, company, or battalion have the training and experience to succeed. Accepting that you are well qualified to command – or will quickly learn what it takes to be effective – is essential to success. You are the one on the ground. No one knows the territory, people, or situation better than the commander on the ground. In combat, the commander tends to apply his learning immediately; experiencing either success or failure, he can quickly correct any errors in the process. On the other hand, micromanaging subordinates distracts junior leaders from their duties and inhibits the development of self-reliant subordinates.

In 1967, despite being an Armor officer, I became the S-3 of an airborne infantry battalion of the 101st Airborne Division at Fort Campbell, Kentucky. We had only three months to train before leaving for Vietnam. After arriving in country, I continued serving as that infantry battalion's operations officer. During that period, I learned under the command of a competent and experienced leader, my battalion commander. There were a number of times when I received a telephone call or a radio message from the commander asking me for all sorts of off-the-wall information. One day, while in his office briefing him on the details of an upcoming operation, I gained an important insight into his seemingly strange behavior. Outside his window was his jeep with the radio tuned to both the brigade and division command frequencies. He was monitoring radio traffic from both superior commanders. As I listened, a call from the division commander demanded from his brigade commanders some detailed information concerning each of their battalions. My battalion commander interrupted my briefing and asked me to get the requested information. When I returned to the battalion commander's office with the information, his telephone was ringing. I handed him a sheet of paper with the required information on it, and he answered the phone call. It was the brigade commander. My battalion commander was able to tell the brigade commander the information he needed.

Later, under extremely difficult conditions, I witnessed this battalion commander display the highest example of mentoring I have seen. It happened on 18 March 1968 while the battalion performed a reconnaissance-in-force mission against enemy forces near Phuoc Vinh, Binh Duong Province. For three days we had slowly beaten our way through heavy undergrowth, demolishing bunkers as we came upon them. In charge of one task force consisting of two infantry companies, I was with the lead company's command section. The battalion commander was with the other two companies on our left

Major Nathaniel F. Colby, 2nd Squadron, 17th Calvary, 1968.

flank. I received a call ordering me to meet him at a one-ship LZ and return to our firebase with him. I had no sooner unloaded my gear than I learned that the infantry company I just left had stumbled into the Dong Ngai Regiment's base camp. Under heavy machine gun and RPG

69

fire, the company had withdrawn into the LZ to set up a circular defense. The battalion commander immediately had his helicopter refueled and headed for the area of operation. As night fell, I was to stand by and expedite any request for assistance from the company in contact. Throughout the night, the battalion commander never left the area. His continual words of comforting reassurance, understanding, and patience with the embattled captain displayed a maturity I remembered for the rest of my life. He didn't tell the captain what to do, nor did he criticize or condemn; he only offered assistance and support. I funneled support in the form of gunships, artillery and tactical air, which the company commander skillfully employed as wave after wave of the enemy, sensing blood, attacked the encircled force.

That night, this young West Point captain earned the Medal of Honor for his valor. I credit the success of the battalion commander to the freedom of action he permitted a young leader in the thick of the battle to call the shots. This battalion commander who, by the way, personally knew each and every one of the company commanders and platoon leaders and their families, retired with three stars on his shoulder after enjoying a most successful career.

We saw combat continually for the next month in Vietnam. At the end of that time, nearly all the officers in the battalion were reassigned. I became the G-3 operations officer at the division headquarters, and as such, I gave the daily G-3 briefings. In April of 1968, I was giving the morning briefing to the commanding general and reported that the division's cavalry squadron was in heavy contact and had taken many casualties over several days. With the squadron commander currently on R&R, the XO was in charge. After the briefing, I received a telephone call from the chief of staff, who told me to pack my bags. I was being reassigned. The chief told me the CG had noticed my Armor brass and concluded that I could probably be better utilized commanding the cavalry squadron in the absence of its commander. Delighted to once again be serving in a troop unit, I caught a helicopter that delivered me to the squadron's brigade headquarters. I was told the brigade commander would talk to me before I assumed command of the squadron firebase. I waited for the brigade commander for several hours. It was getting late in the day, and I wanted to observe the unit in daylight, given the fact that it had experienced a series of night attacks. I finally told the brigade operations officer that I needed to get to my new unit and would speak to the brigade commander when he had an opportunity to visit the firebase.

I left for the firebase by the first available transportation. Late in the afternoon, as I supervised the construction of the overhead cover and defensive positions, the brigade commander arrived by helicopter. I met him and escorted him around. He chewed me up one side and down the other about the firebase's sloppy firing positions. I informed him that the first thing I needed to do was to ensure that the troops had overhead cover and good fighting positions and that the next day we would beautify the area. He stormed off in a fury, evidently satisfied that he had laid the foundation for disciplinary action in the event that we experienced problems during the night.

Two of the squadron's three troops, as well as the mortar platoon, occupied the firebase. It also had a platoon of Army tanks, a platoon of Marine tanks, a platoon of Marine Onthos, and a platoon of Amtracs. The Onthos were lightly armored vehicles with six 106-mm recoilless rifles; the Amtracs mounted a .50 caliber machine gun. Both took their places on the perimeter. The Marine lieutenant commanding the tank platoon had never seen a Starlight scope, and I provided him with one of ours. I also shifted some of the 90-mm Beehive ammunition from the Army tanks to his. The Beehive round, an anti-personnel munition, is filled with thousands of inch-long steel darts. They can be devastating to exposed troops, as we proved that night.

During the night, the platoon leader showed his bravery and coolness under fire by holding his fire until the exact moment when the attacking sappers aimed RPGs at the tanks. Watching the incoming sappers through the Starlight scope, he initiated the defensive attack with a full volley of his 90-mm Beehive rounds and the .30 caliber coaxial mounted machine guns and turret mounted .50 caliber machine guns, while the rest of cavalry squadron and the Amtracs laid down a tremendous fire screen. The two RPG rounds fired at us flashed over the firebase like flares as the Beehive rounds hit the sappers. Our counter-mortar radar spotted the enemy mortar positions, and the mortar platoon hit them dead on. Our action overwhelmed the attackers.

At daybreak the next morning, we could make out multiple bodies and wounded enemy on our protective wire. I did a quick count and found that we had no casualties. We had won a victory at no cost to us. As we extracted the enemy dead and prepared the enemy wounded for medical evacuation by helicopter, the assistant division commander (ADC) arrived. He and I toured the firebase, and he went away well pleased with our successful firefight. Later on, I recommended the Marine tank platoon leader for the Silver Star and personally carried it to his battalion headquarters.

Later in the day, the brigade commander made his appearance at the firebase. He seemed happy and displayed no indication of his anger of the previous day. He made no comments on the fortifications, nor did he apologize for his hard words of the previous day. Obviously, the ADC had made a favorable report on our combat action. The lesson here is to apologize to a subordinate when you are wrong; it is not a sign of weakness; it is a sign of a confident and effective leader.

As a senior commander, one must listen to the junior commander who is closest to the troops, closest to the enemy, and closest to combat reality. Squadron and battalion command posts (CPs) must remain in contact with higher headquarters, complying with reporting responsibilities that can be distracting. The result is a tendency for the commander to remain at his CP, which can be counterproductive. The senior commander must communicate at least two levels below to ascertain the situation on the ground. Division commanders must communicate directly and personally with battalion commanders. Battalion commanders must communicate with platoon leaders on a personal basis. Skip chains of command. Listen to the units in contact with the enemy, talk with them, and get to know them. They will never let you down.

When the cavalry squadron commander returned, I witnessed several instances of the brigade commander micro-managing the squadron commander over the radio in the midst of a combat operation. He told the squadron commander what to do and how to do it during every aspect of an operation. The ADC finally interrupted the radio harassment and informed the brigade commander, over the air, to get off the radio and let the squadron commander do his job. I thought the world of that ADC. He was a leader the troops greatly admired.

I encouraged my junior officers to be independent. I knew they would keep me informed. This takes a great degree of trust. Even when they resorted to a degree of insubordination, I tended to be gentle with them. I knew they had a great passion for their responsibilities. Some senior commanders do not understand the need for such trust and confidence. They regard trust as a loss of control in the unit. They simply did not understand. Their junior officers would have fought and died for their units. By encouraging independence, I was able to break their dependence on their immediate commander for the solution to every situation, and they found confidence in their ability to command.

In the mid-seventies I served as a battalion commander in the

European theater during the period before the lessons learned from our Vietnam experience could be formalized and placed into action. Senior commanders were preoccupied with paperwork and demonstrated a decided tendency to micro-manage subordinates. It made little difference if the unit had any tanks operable so long as the paperwork was straight. Too many senior officers regarded combat readiness as dependent upon valid requisitions for repair parts. Unfortunately, they could do little to correct the long delivery time for replacement of these parts.

What is the appropriate response to a superior who micro-manages subordinates without providing commensurate assistance? How should the subordinate commander respond to what may appear as harassment? The answer is courageous confrontation. Will confrontation end your career? It certainly could. But the goal of the officer corps is not simply to get promoted, which can lead to an unhealthy concern for pleasing the boss. A far more healthy approach to command is to focus on the needs of subordinates, always keeping in mind the legendary caution of General Douglas MacArthur to remember Duty, Honor, Country. It is far better to challenge than to weakly submit to overbearing superiors. If a matter of honor or duty intervenes in the situation, it is essential to stand up for your unit. Never be timid in seeking justice – either for yourself or more importantly for your troops. Justice for your troops is, in the long run, justice for yourself, which your commitment to the Army and the country demands.

A good commander appreciates subordinates with the courage to stand up for the troops and for what they believe is right. If the senior officer doesn't respect honest confrontation, he is not worthy of his authority. The commander who stands up for the troops is worthy of much more – and your men will know it. Officers have a sworn duty to carry out the orders of their superiors, but that doesn't necessarily mean they should pattern their actions after leadership detrimental to the mission.

When my successor gave up command of the tank battalion to an officer who had previously been a troop commander in the squadron in which I had served in Vietnam, I felt very heartened. That battalion later provided the first tanks to enter Baghdad during Operation Enduring Freedom. Our coaching and mentoring of junior leaders to foster independent thought and confidence in their ability to command facilitated their success.

The superior commander who habitually interferes in the running of units in the command may be uncomfortable in his or her current position, therefore resorting to doing what feels more comfortable, usurping command prerogatives of the units at a lower level. Command interference, or micromanagement, reflects poor coaching of the commander in earlier commands, stunting his professional development. Regrettably, poor leadership that fails to foster responsible junior leaders tends to be self-perpetuating. Trust is the key to developing responsible leaders.

A Failure of Courage
by Colonel Alan B. Phillips, USA (Ret.)

Cowards die many times before their deaths;
the valiant never taste of death but once.
— Shakespeare: Julius Caesar

In 1967 I served as commanding officer (CO) of Alpha Company, 4th Battalion, 503rd Airborne Infantry of the 173rd Airborne Brigade in Vietnam. The battalion — conducting search and destroy missions in thick, mountainous, jungle terrain — was operating on this occasion with three companies deployed so as to provide mutual support. Alpha Company led the battalion formation with two rifle companies in trail a thousand meters or so behind. Our mission, based on radio intercepts at least twelve hours old, was to find and destroy an NVA unit reported to be operating in the area.

I deployed my company in column as we began cautiously ascending a mountain that dominated the hilly terrain of the region. Our initial objective was to clear the high ground and laager for the night. The company command post (CP) followed the point platoon and consisted of me, the first sergeant, radio operator, forward observer parties, and a messenger-runner from each rifle platoon. The reserve platoon followed one terrain feature to the rear, three to six hundred meters behind the main body.

With a rainy overcast restricting visibility, the point platoon made contact with an entrenched NVA force shortly before sunset. The platoon leader reported that he was pinned down and taking casualties. Foul weather and darkness ruled out air support, and I directed the forward observers to get the mortars and artillery firing on the enemy positions. I then attempted to raise the reserve platoon leader to direct him to come forward to reinforce our assault, but the radio operator could not make contact with him. I told the reserve platoon runner to run back to his platoon leader with instructions to hurry forward and deploy to the flank to relieve pressure on the lead platoon. Even as indirect fires were adjusted, the firefight intensified, and the lead platoon leader reported more casualties.

When the runner returned, he first reported that he could not locate his platoon, but then emotionally crumbled and admitted he had been too terrified to run back to the platoon. Less than five minutes had elapsed. Meanwhile, the reserve platoon leader, unable to make radio contact, valiantly seized the initiative and marched to the sound of the guns. The appearance of infantry reinforcements on the flank of the contact forced the enemy to withdraw.

Meanwhile, NVA mortar fire had hit the battalion CP, which marched behind Bravo Company, killing the XO, the task force commander. The reserve company commander simultaneously sustained serious injuries. Soon thereafter orders came for Alpha Company to withdraw to the reserve company's position, and I was directed to organize and consolidate the remaining elements of the task force and prepare for further action.

Alpha Company withdrew as ordered and set up defensive positions. While the company prepared its fighting positions, I went in search of the reserve company and found the company XO and first sergeant hugging the bottom of a foxhole. I directed them both to get off their asses and assist my first sergeant in redistributing ammunition, organizing a defense, and accounting for the killed, wounded, and missing. Both men challenged my authority to give them an order and refused to budge during the entire night. In the absence of orders, the junior leaders of the company had taken the initiative to establish firing positions, and I put a second lieutenant platoon leader in temporary command of the company. He did a heroic job, for which he received a DSC. The medics treated dozens of wounded soldiers, and the troops began to hack an LZ out of the jungle in order to permit helicopter evacuation of the wounded.

As the acting task force CO, I directed the consolidation of the night defensive position and the triage of the wounded, while reestablishing a working chain of command based upon the brave junior leaders who had taken control of the situation during the contact.

With the arrival of the battalion commander and sergeant major at daylight, we began lifting out the dead and wounded. We also received reinforcements and reorganized the unit in anticipation of new missions.

The question that confronted the reconstituted chain of command was how to deal with the acts of cowardice that had occurred during the combat of the previous day. In two separate incidents, a total of three men had failed to obey a lawful order and displayed cowardice. I was faced with pressing court martial charges against a soldier in Alpha Company; the battalion commander had to determine what action to take regarding the incident involving a very senior noncommissioned officer and a commissioned officer.

During my investigation, I spoke with the reserve platoon leader whose runner had failed to carry out an order during the contact. We were both struck by the fact that the runner was overcome by remorse for having let down his fellow troopers. A drafted soldier, he had volunteered for duty on the front line and served well. He wanted to do what he had been told but could not muster the required courage. Realizing that the memory of this incident would forever haunt the man, I decided against taking any formal action. Despite the fact that the case against the man was clear-cut, I felt that criminal prosecution would destroy him and do nothing to assist in rebuilding the unit. He remained in the platoon and faithfully soldiered on in some of the toughest combat of the war.

Captain Alan B. Phillips, 4th Battalion, 503rd Airborne Infantry, 1967.

The two other individuals presented a more difficult case. Both men had been openly defiant and cowardly, publicly flouting the standards of military discipline and combat leadership. They were relieved for cause and transferred to rear echelon jobs far from the front lines. Their efficiency reports for the period likely precluded the possibility of future service as combat infantry leaders. To save embarrassment to the battalion, the two never faced courts martial.

In respect to them, I felt justice was not served. Relief for cause and dismissal from the 173rd Airborne Brigade with the stigma of cowardice under fire constituted significant, though not fully satisfactory, retribution. The battalion's engagement in hard fighting at the time may also have played a role in the decision to rid the unit of the cowards at once in lieu of retaining them under guard and conducting a formal court martial during combat operations.

What lessons can we draw from the incident? During our military careers we are called upon to make decisions with great impact upon the lives of our soldiers and must temper those decisions with sound judgment. It would have been easy to recommend court martial charges against the Alpha Company runner. The soldier would have felt the full force of the Uniform Code of Military Justice, while the subsequent decision of the brigade commander to fire the shirkers and banish them from the command in lieu of a court marshal would have set a bad precedent in the unit – harsh treatment of a junior enlisted soldier as opposed to leniency for more senior members of the command. That outcome would have troubled my conscience and failed to serve justice.

Facing Hatred on the Home Front

by Colonel Andrew P. O'Meara, Jr., USA (Ret.)

I still recall the feelings of shock I experienced upon my reception in the United States as we were unloaded from a C-141 Medical Evacuation Flight. While we were being carried on litters down the rear ramp of the aircraft, we who were wounded experienced our first exposure to the insults and hatred of the protestors. War protestors carrying signs that read "BABY KILLERS" and "MURDERERS" lined the tarmac. Dressed in rags – the remnants of Army uniforms – they shouted curses and insults at each of us as we were lifted one at a time down the ramp to waiting buses and ambulances parked nearby to receive the wounded.

We were all shocked. Though aware that some Americans opposed the war, nothing had prepared us for profane taunts and curses. We had given the country our most precious possessions – our lives, our youth, our health, and our buddies. In return, we faced vilification from the only Americans who cared enough to meet soldiers the country and its elected leaders had sent off to war. In that moment, the war's protestors spat upon and cursed the priceless gift of our service to the United States.

Had we been warned of the personal attacks and insults, we could have psychologically prepared ourselves for what we might face. Totally unaware of what to expect and elated by our return home, our joy instead made us especially vulnerable. In those crazy moments on the tarmac, elation quickly turned to confusion, numbness, and anger. There is a lesson to be learned from our humiliation. Just as leaders prepare their soldiers for what they might face in combat, they must also ready them for what they might find when returning home.

In the hectic days of protest — when antiwar radicals picketed recruiters and Army ROTC instructors and called them murderers — the need for other lessons soon emerged. I was there and I bare witness. I soon learned that many Americans opposed the draft and recruitment of soldiers; some universities would no longer tolerate the presence of ROTC on campus; and large numbers of students at many universities showed little restraint in expressing their opposition to the war and all those who wore our nation's uniform.

In universities and across the nation, the strong, the well educated, and those exempt from military service cursed the weak, and the weak remained undefended and uncomprehending. Powerless to respond, I read newspaper accounts denouncing the war. From my combat service in Vietnam, I knew that the curses of the influential and powerful were undeserved and that resisting ruthless attacks by North Vietnam upon the South Vietnamese population was truly a just cause, as President Kennedy had made clear in his inaugural address. Despite what the media reported, our soldiers fought a just war in defense of liberty, and they waged it morally.

Those who believed otherwise challenged all who publicly wore the uniform in America. Bitter knowledge, indeed, but important for leaders to understand and share with soldiers seeking to do their duty on the home front. Most important of all, leaders needed to convey to their soldiers that when confronted by misguided protestors, they must not retaliate. They must exercise self-control and continue to do their duty with honor and dignity.

Those of us wearing the uniform with pride had to learn how to respond if spat upon. We had to practice turning the other cheek when flower children placed flowers in the weapons of soldiers under arms, while others threw human waste upon uniforms worn with pride. We had to remain calm and step over the inert bodies of demonstrators who physically blocked the entrances to office buildings and teaching facilities. We had to find the moral courage to do our duty under circumstances that can only be described as humiliating and inexcusable.

The Vietnam conflict touched virtually all Americans. Along with other social forces, it set in motion a cultural upheaval and spawned an antiwar movement that formed a chasm within and between generations. From a political perspective, it also created bitter opposition within and between political parties, leaving a legacy of animosity not seen since the end of the Civil War. In some ways, the legacy of the war still casts its shadow over the political landscape, creating sharp differences within the generation that participated in the great events of the period. What the antiwar movement saw and remembered as courageous, their opponents viewed as outrageous. Labels of heroes and turncoats were ascribed to the selfsame actors revealing the depth of the deep split in the culture — a split over a war that ended in tragedy that still touches the souls of my generation.

What became the opposition to the war in Vietnam had deep and diverse roots in organizations and movements far older than the conflict in Southeast Asia, and their purposes sometimes seemed only remotely related to the war. By the mid-sixties the conflict in Vietnam had nevertheless drawn some Americans into a too often violent and often illegal opposition to the war. Though by the sixties the American peace movement had existed for a century, the Cold War produced new and more radical advocates of peace, such as the National Committee for a Sane Nuclear Policy (SANE). Labor and socialist bodies of almost equal age had by the Sixties spun off a New Left and organizations such as Students for a Democratic Society (SDS). In time even advocates of civil rights came to believe that the war impeded their efforts and must, therefore, be terminated.

Other opponents were less organized but often very influential. In 1962, Indochina expert Bernard Fall, author of *Street Without Joy*, prompted *The New Republic* to issue a special issue of that weekly magazine under the headline "No Win in Vietnam." Two years later, prominent political scientist and strategist Hans Morganthau had helped organize a SANE petition calling for the neutralization of Vietnam's two halves. Within the government, Under Secretary of State George Ball, appointed by President John Kennedy, described the war to President Lyndon Johnson as not winnable and opposed sending combat units to Vietnam. Two U. S. Senators opposed the 1964 Tonkin Gulf Resolution authorizing that escalation, and four members of the Senate Foreign

Relations Committee, including its chairman J. William Fulbright, later urged repeal of the resolution. Nearly four decades after my return to the United States, I still recall the feelings of shock I experienced upon my reception at Travis Air Force Base in 1969 while being carried on a litter from the rear ramp of a C-141 Medical Evacuation Flight returning wounded soldiers from Vietnam.

Many academicians, intellectuals, and statesmen had thus come to regard the war as a mistake. The wider response to Johnson's decision to bomb North Vietnam and send American combat troops to the South soon gave opposition to the war greater strength and a new character and led to excesses that both harmed the war effort and so injured members of the armed forces — the behavior that I described earlier in this essay.

In response to the bombing, sociologist William Gamson, a leader within the Congress of Racial Equality, met with fifteen University of Michigan faculty members to plan cancellation of classes for a one-day "teach-in" on the war, an idea that soon spread to dozens of other universities. The teach-ins also linked members of the traditional peace movement with both university faculty and students. In April 1965, the politically radical SDS shifted its focus and held its first demonstration in the nation's capital, helping to draw the New Left into the antiwar movement. The Free Speech Movement at the University of California in Berkeley and similar movements elsewhere also shifted their attention from civil rights to opposing the war in Vietnam. The number and size of the antiwar demonstrations quickly grew. Three hundred thousand gathered in New York City in 1967 and a hundred thousand at the Pentagon later the same year.

As the number of American troops in Vietnam rose — along with the number of casualties — members of the clergy and business community also began to question the war. Following the Tet Offensive of 1968, the media began to editorialize against as well as report on the war. The Cambodian invasion of 1970 and the shooting, by National Guardsmen, of demonstrating students at Kent State University and Jackson State University further fueled protests that became increasingly violent.

Many of those opposing the war had crossed the line, going violently beyond peaceful assembly and a call for the redress of grievances. They also inexcusably made those who served in the armed forces special targets for their anger and abuse. From my perspective as an Army ROTC instructor with previous combat experience in Vietnam, the scions of the establishment—the most-favored sons—teed off on the draft Army, the scions of working families and middle-class Americans. Those who served out of great need with aspirations for a better tomorrow were utterly defenseless—inarticulate, unlettered, and without comprehension — and without an advocate before the court of public opinion, which had been prejudiced against them without concern for those who bore the burdens of national defense. The strong cursed the weak, and the weak were defenseless and uncomprehending.

To military professionals, the courage of self-sacrifice epitomizes virtue – the love of duty and honor beyond self-love – and entails living for a noble cause, and if need be, dying in an act of selfless service. We recently observed the nobility of total self-sacrifice in the deeds of the NYPD and the NYFD during the horrifying events of 9/11. These were servants of the public laying down their lives while attempting to save those in desperate need. We see the same self-sacrifice in the actions of men and women in uniform fighting to defeat terrorists in Iraq and Afghanistan. Such deeds have historically become an example to all generations through the power of self-sacrifice, enshrining the memory of the dead for the ages. For a time, opposition to the war in Vietnam tragically hid the grandeur of such courage.

The lesson learned by those of us who confronted the antiwar movement on the home front during the Vietnam War was that our duty is to conduct ourselves with dignity despite grave provocation. Our obligation to support troops in harm's way can only succeed by carrying out our mission while respecting the rights of our fellow citizens to practice the liberties enumerated in the Bill of Rights. When radical opposition seeking to prevent soldiers from performing their duty violates the law at home, we must rely upon the civil authorities to maintain law and order. Moreover, as leaders of soldiers returning from combat on foreign soil, it is our duty to prepare our service men and women for possible provocations by the opposition – one of the prices we pay for the privilege of service in uniform. Had we understood the potential impact of the attacks upon unwary soldiers returning from Vietnam, many of whom were gravely injured in battle, we might have been able to prevent the psychological trauma experienced by many who were totally unprepared for the unfounded attacks upon their service and personal honor.

A Problem of Loyalty

by Lieutenant Colonel William L. Schwartz, USA (Ret.)

A conflict between a junior officer's loyalty to a commander and his professional responsibility to the unit and soldiers who make up the command creates a very difficult position, one more challenging than having to deal with an obviously illegal order. In the following article, Major Schwartz shares such a conflict and his difficult decision as he sought to do his duty, preserve the welfare of the command and accomplish the mission of the unit.
– The Editors

Loyalty, an inherent obligation of all leaders, has three dimensions:

loyalty to one's immediate superior; loyalty to one's subordinates; and loyalty to the Army and the nation it defends. In most instances, junior officers have little difficulty reconciling the three. Though thankfully rare, occasions do arise when loyalty to one's subordinates, the mission, and the Army seemingly conflict with the loyalty due one's immediate superior – and no amount of respectful disagreement can resolve the problem. Especially in combat, when lives are at risk and time for discussion is limited, those situations often produce a professional crisis in which the officer feels that he must put his career and his professional reputation at risk, choose to disobey his superior's orders, and thereby better serve the unit's mission and protect the lives of its soldiers. In some cases, the junior may so act believing he has a better understanding of the situation and confident that his superior, when better informed, will likely approve the junior's rejection of an order. In other cases, the truly difficult ones, the junior must believe that, in a situation well known to both, his professional judgment is better than that of his superior.

In the fall of 1970, I became the Executive Officer of a well-trained airmobile infantry battalion with a fine combat record and history and traditions stretching back over a hundred years. A demanding but fair commander, supported by an excellent staff, then led the battalion. With few exceptions, the officers assigned to the companies performed admirably, and except for one junior commander, all the officers in the battalion had a minimum four months of experience in their jobs.

As the time for departure of the battalion commander drew near, ugly rumors regarding his replacement reached the unit. Many of the battalion's NCOs, who had previously worked for the man, requested transfers. The "word" described the new commander as an uncaring officer with a history of rash decisions resulting in needless casualties. Nor was the incoming commander branch qualified, despite the fact

86

that he had previously commanded an infantry battalion in another brigade. Rumor had it that he owed his previous position, as well as his forthcoming command of our battalion, to the influence of the corps commander.

Soon after the arrival of our new commander, Lieutenant Colonel Smith (a pseudonym), we found the rumors well founded. Smith proved to be an arrogant, brash man, grossly inconsiderate of his subordinates, a contempt he publicly aired on the battalion's command frequency. Even more troubling, his subordinates soon discovered his dishonesty and total lack of the basic integrity required of a military professional.

Further complicating the situation, the new commander had a drinking problem, and his soldiers often observed him drunk on the firebase and, worse yet, drinking with his subordinates. The bad example of the commander resulted in inebriated NCOs and officers. In short, Smith was unprofessional in his relationships with his subordinates and he was a borderline alcoholic.

Whether it involved airmobile operations or the employment of infantry in jungle terrain, Smith demonstrated a seriously deficient knowledge of basic infantry tactics, and his poor judgments led to casualties. His administrative decisions were no better than his tactical judgments; for example, he reassigned officers from job to job so often that many received no efficiency reports for their time in the unit. He attempted to court martial troops who contracted malaria, even when they had contracted a form of the disease not amenable to prophylaxis. In sum, he was a bad commander who made a mockery of basic leadership techniques. Needless to say, an incompetent leader in command of an infantry battalion in combat endangered the lives of the troops and hurt the morale of a previously excellent unit.

The incompetence of the battalion commander soon became known at brigade headquarters. With the brigade commander clearly displeased with Smith's performance, members of the brigade staff informed me to expect Smith's relief in the near future. Even so, while the battalion coped with a poor commander, the brigade commander delayed Smith's relief.

Despite the brigade commander's lack of confidence in Smith, he assigned the battalion to a new area of operations, which required moving the firebase. A challenging movement even for a competent commander, that mission posed a difficult test for a less than able officer. The brigade S-3 told me that the brigade commander had decided that if the move went badly, he would relieve Smith, a decision confirmed by the brigade executive officer.

After Smith presented his planning guidance for the move to the S-3 and me, it became clear to both of us that the switch to a new firebase, always risky, could not be properly and safely accomplished based on the commander's guidance. In response to his technically and tactically unsound views, we offered suggestions based on experience we had gained from two previous firebase relocations. Smith scornfully rejected our advice, leaving us no choice but to begin implementing his faulty planning guidance. As we proceeded, it became obvious to the entire battalion staff that the battalion was about to blunder – and badly at that.

Two days prior to the move, Smith informed me that he was removing himself from the planning process and would be out of the AO on the day of the move. He then placed the entire operation in my hands.

The S-3 and I consequently faced a fundamental dilemma: Execute a relocation plan based on our commander's faulty planning guidance, confidently believing that doing so would produce failure and predictably result in Smith's relief? Or revise the plans in the absence of Smith and conduct the move properly, leaving the battalion to continue coping with its incompetent leader?

If we executed the firebase move as originally planned, the S-3 and I had good reason to believe that doing so would endanger elements of the unit. Equally aggravating was the knowledge that the flawed command guidance would result in an operational and logistical mess. Were these risks worth running, we asked, if the outcome would rid the battalion of a commander whose daily presence endangered the battalion? We had several hours to make up our minds.

Smith had placed me in charge of the operation, and the S-3 now worked directly for me. I could not bring myself knowingly to allow bad guidance to botch up the operation. We decided to conduct the

Major William L. Schwartz, 1st Cavalry Division (Air Mobile), 1970.

operation the best way we knew, applying our professional knowledge and the lessons learned during the successful conduct of our previous firebase moves. We based our decision on two considerations: First, we had a responsibility to the Army, to our division,

and, most importantly, to the men of the battalion to do our best to ensure that we completed the move as effectively as possible. Second, our professional and personal pride would not permit us to settle for anything less than our best.

Moving a firebase, always a challenging task, takes most of a day and roughly 55 Chinook helicopter loads of troops, artillery pieces, weapons, ammunition and equipment. While the move went ahead, we constantly had to compress the battalion's old defensive perimeter as loads and troops went out – a job we must complete before the enemy could react. Imperatively, the last load must go out before dark. Our plan called for the S-3 to move to the new firebase with the first lift. I would remain at the old firebase and go out on our command and control (C&C) helicopter with my communications team after the last Chinook left.

Using our plan, the battalion efficiently and safely executed the move to the new firebase, although an unanticipated problem arose as we were completing the move. When the last Chinook load lifted out, I waited with five troopers for the S-3 to send C&C bird for us as planned. With night coming on and no helicopter in sight, I became increasingly anxious. I finally went up on the guard frequency, found a helicopter with the brigade S-3 on board, and asked him to get us out. When I arrived at the new firebase, angry about being stranded, I discovered the reason. Smith had returned and seeing that the last Chinook had landed, he cancelled the last flight going to the old firebase. Failing to perceive there might have been a good reason for the C&C helicopter to return to the old base, Smith made no effort to check with the battalion S-3 and left me and five of his men stranded and almost defenseless. Despite the difficulties created by Smith's cancellation of our final evacuation helicopter, the operation had succeeded. We had done our duty and the unit had performed well – an outcome that saved Smith from a predicted relief for cause.

Major Schwartz used his professional judgment to correct an absent commander's flawed guidance, resulting in the safe movement of the unit into its new area of operation and the establishment of a new fire base. The decision to override the flawed instructions of an incompetent commander required confident leadership.
— The Editors

Rebuilding a Vital Combat Service Support Unit

by Colonel Donald R. Reinhard, USA (Ret.)

You may someday discover one of your most rewarding experiences in what you initially regarded as a doubtful assignment. In 1967, the 191st Ordnance Battalion (AMMO) certainly seemed such a place, an exhausted and under strength unit facing enormous demands with me, a most unlikely executive officer, for the unit. Six months and many changes later, experience had taught me that important lesson about new assignments as well many others.

To be sure, the 191st Ordnance Battalion did not have the look of a plum assignment. In many respects a sick unit, it had only one way to go–UP! Initially tasked to back up the main ammunition depots in Vietnam—the 3rd & 184th Ordnance Battalions—the Army had formed the 191st from scratch at Fort Sill using an experienced cadre and soldiers fresh from the Ordnance Ammunition School at Huntsville, Alabama, in 1966. By the summer of 1967, the second generation of replacements began arriving. Most were soldiers who lacked training as ammunition technicians, all those with experience already being in-country. The mission also changed, making the battalion a significant retail source for nearby tactical units as well as support for a far-flung network of smaller ammo supply points ranging from Da Nang, several hundred miles north, to Phan Thiet, about 100 miles to the south. An army at peace had not required a large force of ammo handlers to move high volumes of munitions; when wartime demand exploded, it suffered from a paucity of those who knew the work. By the time I arrived, fewer than 75% of the members of the battalion's three under-strength ammo companies had a military occupation specialty (MOS) that matched their job. One of the companies had little more than a cadre of unqualified replacements acting as a chain of command.

The records of several of the battalion's previous leaders also painted an unattractive picture. I quickly learned that due to a gross inventory error that resulted in a zero balance of 40mm grenades, the Army had relieved a company commander and the battalion's materiel officer (a major, responsible for accomplishing the technical mission as opposed to the S-3, a captain, responsible for all other operations). With an inventory error rate of more than fifty percent, the battalion was fortunate to have no zero balances in other vital ammunition as well, and its commander likely would have faced relief had he not left Vietnam before discovery of the inventory debacle.

If the 191st Ordnance Battalion did not look like a prize assignment, neither would a disinterested observer have selected someone with my background to assist in its recovery. After two unproductive years in Air Defense Artillery, a graduate degree in electrical engineering, a year on the White Sands Missile Range, a branch transfer, and a three-year Ordnance teaching assignment at West Point, I found myself, lacking any training in the Ordnance Corps' ammunition mission and thrust into the battalion's XO slot in the middle of a shooting war. The exact words from my assignments officer provided little encouragement: "Learn the job through OJT [on the job training]. This is the place where we figure you can do the least damage." It sounded like a vote of no confidence in a successful assignment to the Army in the field!

I soon learned that the Army's ammunition handlers, MOS 55B— "ammo humpers" in the vernacular—had an ill-deserved reputation for being all brawn and no brain. The operations tempo required that the 191st move fifty tons of ammunition per hour, 24/7. It received ammo from cargo ships and aircraft, loaded line-haul convoy trailers, prepared air shipments, and dispatched ammunition to the port for intra-coastal movement. Like members of all field units, ammo handlers worked in the typical hot, humid conditions of South Vietnam. Even with the aid of forklifts and cranes, troops were physically beat by the end of a shift.

The 191st and those it supported literally lived or died by what was done or not done by privates whose physically demanding jobs seldom earned them any glory or recognition of their daily challenges. Soldiers holding 55B MOS had to know the compatibilities of various kinds of ammunition and honor stringent safety measures in order to prevent accidents – one of which could wipe out the entire ammunition inventory in the blink of an eye.

Combined with the physical challenge of the job, the MOS also required first-rate record keeping. The depot held over a hundred thousand tons of munitions consisting of ten million rounds of ammunition in more than a thousand line items produced by over thirty thousand manufacturers, all of which had to be separately accounted for. The job demanded meticulous record keeping – work that brought no glory. The "ammo humpers" had to master inventory methods matched in sensitivity only by medical supply. Ammunition available to combat units is a measure of combat power, just as is numbers of soldiers and weapons; therefore, in terms of quantities and rates of movement, ammunition is measured in hundreds and thousands of tons – orders of magnitude greater than any other class of supply. The soldiers performed all the record keeping in those days with pencil, paper, and Marchant mechanical adding machines.

Training and motivating the troops to accurately count the munitions moving through the depot posed a challenge. It took seven people to form an inventory team; a correct count required counting every item twice by two different people and that the counts match. An added frustration was that the individual counters were not permitted to talk to one another while counting. Counts went into the thousands while doing artillery projectiles and into the millions while doing small arms ammunition. It was mentally demanding as well as backbreaking work.

Prior to the commitment of U. S. ground forces to Vietnam, no one recognized the magnitude of the ammunition requirements to support combat units committed to an insurgency. As we coped with the ever-increasing requirements, the demands on the ammunition units escalated accordingly. In short, the job was exceptionally complex. When I arrived, the demands on the unit had stretched its three ammo companies to the point of exhaustion. With only enough troops to man two companies, personnel managers had resorted to filling the units with anyone available: even clerks, dental assistants, mortuary technicians, and bakers. With the high unit OPTEMPO each company split itself in half in order to operate 24/7. Whatever misgivings I brought to my assignment, working with the "ammo humpers" soon changed my early perceptions to profound respect – another aspect of my first lesson.

The labor service company, which provided security for the depot, was in the worst shape. Except for its staff and platoon sergeants, no soldier held a rank above PFC. The company had only one officer, the CO. Its soldiers had little hope for promotion. The company mess hall was in bad shape. The first sergeant and company commander were marginally effective, and the unit living conditions were deplorable. Their mission was unexciting – standing guard 24/7 in watchtowers. The morale of the labor service company was predictably low. With little prospect for promotion and with poor leadership, its privates nevertheless got the job done. Amazingly, they had a very low Article 15 rate – and they performed an essential function: securing an ammunition-storage area the size of two small towns.

I soon recognized that despite the battalion's shortcomings, the units it served literally lived or died by what was done by the junior members of its four companies. Upon reporting to the 191st, I hit the ground running. I knew nothing about ammunition supply procedures, and the battalion's materiel officer was totally focused on his demanding functions, so the doctrinal split in responsibilities between us was natural and worked very smoothly. He oversaw the mission, and I did the rest. The battalion commander left us alone and took care of his own responsibilities, principally keeping the Cam Ranh Bay Depot off our backs.

To motivate the troops, we of the second-generation officer and NCO leadership really emphasized the ammo humpers' informal motto: "You can live for months without mail; for weeks without food; for days without water; for hours without POL; but you cannot live for seconds without ammo." The battalion learned what had to be done and started figuring out how to do it well, training its soldiers as necessary. It boiled down to instilling a sense of pride in mission accomplishment and high standards of performance. The materiel officer spent a significant amount of time driving around, overseeing operations, hounding the company commanders on deficiencies — and praising them for things done well. Those are basic leadership techniques, but nonetheless they were essential to accomplishing the mission. Outside the battalion, he attended interminable meetings that took official notice of any shortfall in performance but no notice of our accomplishments. From his wanderings within the battalion, however, he knew the situation and witnessed the dramatic improvement in the unit's performance.

My job as XO included everything not covered by the materiel officer. I focused on issues such as security and defense, unit funds, morale items, promotion lists, personnel issues, emergency leaves, training, motor pool management, mess hall improvements, clean up of unit areas, and most important — visiting the battalion's off-site detachments. Like my materiel officer counterpart, I spent half my time driving around the battalion area, seeing the troops, talking with the company commanders, checking the perimeter areas, and with the help of the S-2 keeping a finger on the pulse of the enemy situation. We had some marginal officers — lieutenants in the companies and a captain acting as the S-3 — who also required my supervision. The battalion benefited by the assignment of a trio of imaginative captains commanding the three ammo companies, so we gave them their lead and got out of their way.

Lessons learned in my earlier Air Defense Artillery assignment proved useful. For example, taking care of the troops meant making it known to them that the chain of command would address their individual problems. I took more than one soldier to the Inspector General to discuss some problem that seemed insurmountable to the soldier and nearly impossible for me. Though I did not solve every problem, the troops knew I cared. Except in the labor service company, promotion was possible, and maintenance of a good, equitable, and fair promotion system was a key morale issue.

I reviewed our promotion system with the battalion's command sergeant major (CSM). We discovered some inequities crying out for correction. We quickly fixed the situation and shuffled a few names around on the list for staff sergeant, correcting long-standing inequities in the unit. We made a few soldiers unhappy but our efforts paid off. It goes without saying that we made the best use of the talent available.

The labor service company represented the greatest challenge. With the help of the CSM, I resolved to find a competent first sergeant. We sat down with the battalion commander, convinced him of the need for change and found the right non-commissioned officer for the job. In my travels around the perimeter, I made it a point to visit and chat with all the guards. The new first sergeant put the screws to the company's other sergeants and the company commander backed his new first sergeant. We managed to get them some unit fund money to improve their day room. With the mess hall upgraded, morale went up and performance improved. There was absolutely nothing we could do about the organizational structure, and promotions remained a problem. Even so, the troops could see that the battalion staff looked out for them, respected their contribution, and did what it could to make their lives more pleasant.

The labor service company personnel problem was eventually solved when the personnel command in Vietnam started sending us replacements from combat units — all of whom had at least two Purple Hearts and most of whom had rank. Recovering from wounds, they seemed content to complete their tours in a secure area.

The battalion had previously overlooked many of the humble but essential housekeeping tasks that build effective units. With the ammo humpers well trained and motivated, leading by moving around the depot, getting to know the troops, and working closely with the command sergeant major, I soon observed the 191st begin to move up.

* * * * *

The realities of war came home to the 191st during the Chinese New Year – Tet – at the end of January 1968. During Tet, the North Vietnamese Army and the Viet Cong mounted their most aggressive offensive to date and did so all across South Vietnam. Like many combat units, the 191st found itself ill prepared. Fortunately, I had our S-2, Lieutenant Anderson, checking with every known source of intelligence. We learned that Viet Cong sappers had caused several fires in the other ammo battalions.

Lieutenant Anderson and I had been looking at options to upgrade our security since I arrived in the unit. The week after I arrived, I tasked one of the departing captains with writing an operations order for responding to a sapper attack on the depot. In about three days he presented a reasonable plan, and I had a better appreciation of how to defend the ammunition depot from sappers. He had envisioned an attack from the sea by sappers coming ashore in the wilds of the coast, infiltrating through the thick brushy ravines, and entering our storage areas through the perimeter.

Our depot abutted a white-sand beach that formed a crescent about five miles long. The defense plan given us by the depot commander required more personnel than we could allocate to security and still execute our mission. I knew the staff needed to use its imagination and develop a better plan. So, we tied into the units on the right and left. To our right we had the U. S. Navy and to our left the U. S. Air Force. The Navy patrolled the bay off our beach with Swift boats. The Air Force had established an observation post (OP) with a .50 caliber machine gun equipped with a Starlight night vision scope atop a hill commanding the approaches from the north. We also augmented our security with Military Police who patrolled inside our perimeter with dogs. In addition, we established a strong point with several machine guns on a promontory commanding the approach to the beach. An OP manned by two soldiers with a machine gun covered another exit route off the south end of the beach. Finally, we created a reaction force with vehicles ready to go wherever we found intruders. The battalion commander approved the plan; each company commander received his mission and set out to perform it. Lieutenant Anderson had combat time – and a Purple Heart – as a platoon leader in the 11th Armored Cavalry Regiment, and I relied heavily on him in formulating our response to Tet.

Responding to our defense plan, one of the company commanders reported that he needed a mortar for illumination of the jungle approaches to his storage area. The S-4 procured a mortar — without a sight. Finding a former Infantry sergeant in the unit, he and I made a range card and learned to place the rounds where we wanted them. Once again, I solved problems by getting personally involved, seeking expertise where it might be found, and relying on others.

Believing that lots of activity might provide our best security, we kept operations going at as high a rate as we could. Vehicles were sent over the roads at random times to keep from establishing a pattern. I spent my twenty-hour days wandering the area, visiting the troops, and checking on things. All was secure. Or so we thought.

With the guard successfully posted and the old relief about to return to quarters at about 2200 hours one evening, an MP reported that his dog had alerted on the perimeter. We collected every available soldier with a weapon and went to the far end of the storage area. My instructions were very brief: Fan out and run, on foot, down the depot's roads, examining each ammunition pad as we came to it, especially the rear areas that abutted the jungle undergrowth. If anyone found demolition charges, he had no choice but to grab them and toss them into the jungle. I led the search. Thirty minutes later, having checked the area, things settled down, but we increased our motor patrols in the area. At dawn we re-examined the area and found no signs of enemy activity. Thus ended my "battle" of Cam Ranh Bay in 1968.

My tour had taught me a lot: Don't accept rumors that yours is a bad unit. Lead by walking around. Respect, train, and take care of the troops. Don't think you know it all. Seek advice and assistance from others. Make the best use of the skills available in the unit. Give careful consideration to the counsel of experienced junior officers and senior sergeants. When the school solution seems unworkable, fall back on your imagination and the ingenuity of your soldiers.

Relief for Cowardice

by Colonel Barrett S. Haight, USA (Ret.)

Because relief from command for "failing to engage the enemy" hints at cowardice, it surely ranks amongst the most humiliating fates a young officer can experience. Consider the case of a new lieutenant serving with the 1st Infantry Division in Vietnam in 1969. Setting his men into a night defensive position in a rice paddy, he sited his claymore mines and automatic weapons to cover the direction from which battalion intelligence indicated the enemy might approach and also preplanned supporting fires from the company mortars and the battalion "Duster" – a track mounted 40-mm gun. Suddenly, to his rear and side, a long line of armed North Vietnamese and Viet Cong soldiers appeared, marching at quick time past his position. Though startled, the lieutenant shifted some of his unit's weapons, called for his supporting fires, and prepared to engage. Though he had preplanned the supporting fires, neither the artillery nor the Duster responded to his call. By the time the lieutenant consulted his sergeant and decided nevertheless to reveal their position by firing on the now rapidly disappearing enemy, his unit's fire proved ineffectual against an estimated three-hundred-man enemy unit that had moved within range of its position for only a matter of minutes. The lieutenant's battalion later chased the enemy into "spider" holes, killing many but taking casualties during the engagement.

Based upon initial reports of the lieutenant's actions, the battalion commander relieved him for "failing to engage the enemy." The brigade commander, wanting to support his officers, asked division to investigate. I made that investigation, and it confirmed the facts already described, identifying lapses at several levels – from the lieutenant's actions to the battalion's. I recommended corrective actions and restoration of the

100

lieutenant to command of his platoon.

Offered the opportunity to comment on my findings and recommendations, the battalion commander reinstated the lieutenant, a decision later approved by the brigade commander. In the next few months, the lieutenant redeemed their trust by efficient, aggressive, and valorous actions in several combat operations.

For several reasons, that incident ended favorably:

•The battalion commander, undoubtedly influenced by the deaths of soldiers killed when digging the enemy out of his spider holes, had relieved the lieutenant based on sketchy information. Once fully aware of the situation, he made a better-informed decision to reinstate the lieutenant, which saved the reputation and career of a young officer who later proved himself.

•Reinstatement occurred because the brigade commander ordered a thorough investigation by an experienced officer who took the time to dig the facts out of a complex situation. Just as gathering reliable combat intelligence demands hard, ongoing effort by senior officers and NCOs, so does an investigation of what occurred during an unusual combat operation.

•Having obtained the whole story, the senior commanders could make sound decisions.

Situations such as the well-known "My Lai" incident suggest an additional requirement for achieving a satisfactory outcome: Complex cases require effective investigation. That did not occur immediately following the incident and resulted in the punishment of soldiers and officers up to the grade of major general either for failing to report and investigate or for covering up allegations – later proved true – that U. S. forces had murdered a large number of unarmed civilians in the village of My Lai. During the war in Iraq, the armed forces have also disciplined soldiers and officers for failing to take "appropriate action" regarding misuse of interrogation procedures in the handling of captured enemy suspects.

Rather than ignore possible misconduct, officers at all levels and within their resources must effectively investigate their suspicions and send their findings and recommendations up the chain-of-command lest an inadequate investigation discredit the armed forces and subject them to disgrace. At a minimum, a good investigation is objective, detailed, based on the best available sources, and leads to findings clearly derived from the documented facts

Major Barrett S. Haight, 1st Infantry Division, 1968.

and to recommendations supported by the facts, findings, and applicable law and policies.

The essence of the above "leadership lesson" is that good decisions require good information (all the facts), and good information will lead to good decisions.

FOUR
CHALLENGES *on the* FRONTIERS
of FREEDOM

Defending the Frontiers of Freedom entailed deterring Warsaw Pact aggression by strategic deterrent forces as well as forward deployed forces in the Federal Republic of Germany and along the DMZ in Korea. The mission was demanding, involving the training of units and new leaders. The challenge became more demanding during the war in Vietnam, when the American armed forces encountered opposition to the war on the home front and endured severe funding cuts for the forces defending NATO and operating the Army training base. The cuts drew down these forces to foot the bills entailed in fighting the undeclared war in Southeast Asia. The Congress and the American electorate had been told that the Johnson Administration opposed an expansion of the fighting in Vietnam. Despite pledges to avoid a wider war and running for re-election on a peace platform, President Johnson greatly expanded the war from several thousand advisors and support troops in country at the time of President Kennedy's assassination to over 550,000 troops in South Vietnam at the end of Johnson's term of office. The following leadership vignettes have as their background both training missions and the price the armed forces paid for the austerity measures imposed by Secretary of Defense Robert S. McNamara.
— *The Editors*

Reflections on the Yom Kippur War

by Major General Nicholas Krawciw, USA (Ret.)

Looking back over the span of my military career, I regard an assignment to the Middle East in the early seventies as the most interesting and exciting of my service. Following my nomination for duty with the United Nations, friends and classmates described the assignment as "peripheral," not career enhancing. I followed my instinct, however, and never regretted my decision to do something truly unusual at least once in my career. This is the story of that two-year assignment. In early 1972, the Army detailed me to the United Nations Truce Supervision Organization (UNTSO) in which I served in and around Israel from March 1972 until April 1974, a period that included the October 1973 Yom Kippur War. Although many key events of that war appear here, this account is neither a history of its operations nor of UNTSO. It is the story of my peacekeeping experience during the Cold War on an ancient frontier of civilizations and includes information passed to me during and after the war by colleagues in UNTSO and Arab and Israeli friends. The oldest UN peacekeeping entity, UNTSO, created by the Security Council following the first Arab-Israeli War in 1948-49, received a continuous mandate (does not need to be renewed periodically by the Security Council like most other UN peacekeeping activities). In various capacities, officers of all branches of the U.S. armed forces have participated in the organization from its beginning.

In the fall of 1971, Lieutenant General Richard Stilwell, the U.S. Army Deputy Chief of Staff for Operations, nominated me to the UN Military Committee to be the next Chief Operations Officer (COO) of UNTSO. The job description called for a combat arms officer with no background in military intelligence. After months of waiting for my acceptance by Israel and its Arab neighbors, their approval came in January of 1972. My family and I began preparing for our trip to the Middle East. After a very pleasant three weeks leave in Greece and Crete, where we visited Minoan ruins and World War II battlefields, we arrived in Jerusalem in March. I reported to UNTSO headquarters at Government House, the British headquarters in Palestine before 1949, and was welcomed by the organization's Chief of Staff (the UN title for the de facto commanding general), Major General Ensio Siilasvuo, a World War II veteran of the Finnish Army. Other greetings and briefings came in rapid succession: Colonel Bunworth, Irish Army, Senior Staff Officer (SSO) and in fact the organization's chief of staff; other members of the staff; and the outgoing COO, Lieutenant Colonel Gay Dunham, U.S. Army. As I recall, some 230 officers from sixteen nations served as unarmed observers manning observation posts (OPs) along the cease-fire lines established following the 1967 Arab-Israeli War. Each contributing nation kept a certain number of observers assigned to UNTSO. Some nations, such as Ireland and Finland, maintained up to 36 officers in the mission. Others, including the United States, kept much smaller numbers. I soon became the senior officer of a U.S. Military Observer group of eight Americans from all services of our armed forces. My duties included administrative, logistic, and disciplinary responsibilities. A large staff of "UN Field Service" logisticians, communicators, administrators, medics, and transportation specialists supported my group. Before taking over my COO duties in mid-May, plans called for

Lieutenant Colonel Nicholas Krawciw, UN Truce Supervision Organization, alongside immobilized Syrian tanks, 1973.

me to become familiar with the cease-fire lines overseen by UNTSO. As a result, I served at selected OPs on the Golan Heights and along the Suez Canal. UNTSO had over twenty such posts along each of the two lines. Since the 1967 War, the Suez Canal had marked the line between Egypt and Israel, and a strip of no-man's land separating the Israeli and Syrian armies at the end of that war served as the line between those two nations.

My familiarization first took me to OPs on the Golan Heights, which abut the Mount Hermon range lying between Lebanon and Syria. The Israelis controlled great defensive positions on the northeastern part of the Heights, which contains small hills and deserted Druse villages. The terrain, although rocky in places, provided for easy mobility of armored vehicles. No-man's land, nearer Mount Hermon, stretched some 70 kilometers to the south and southwest. Its width varied from a few hundred meters in the north and south to 1,600 meters in the center near the ruins of the Druse town of Kuneitra. The Yarmouk Canyon, impassible for armor but not infantry, constituted the southern and southeastern part of the area between cease-fire lines. Since 1967 the Israelis kept their armored units in the center and the north of the Golan Heights and lighter infantry units in the south. Both sides placed extensive minefields in front of their positions.

Like other observers, I was paired with an officer from another nation, and we drove out to a designated Golan Heights OP, carrying with us supplies for six days. At each OP, the outgoing pair of observers briefed us before we assumed our duties observing the cease-fire lines and reporting by radio any violations, such as movement or fires across the lines—to include military overflights. Reports from OPs on the Israeli side of the lines went to the Tiberias Control Station, which collated and forwarded them to UNTSO headquarters in Jerusalem. They then went to the UN in Geneva and on to New York, where they were published as Security Council documents. The reports from the OPs on the Syrian side of the lines went to UNTSO's control station in Damascus before going to Jerusalem, Geneva, and New York.

Each OP on the Golan Heights contained a living-observation trailer and a pyramidal granite stone bunker; we took turns doing housekeeping and observing. The Druse, indigenous people of the Golan Heights, had built the bunkers, which saved many observer lives during the Yom Kippur War. From the OP we could see nearby Israeli and Syrian positions and watch Israeli patrols and other activities along their side of the line. The most interesting OPs were in vicinity of the old Druze town of Kuneitra, which straddled the Tiberias-to-Damascus highway and contained the Israeli forward command post and both infantry and armor battle positions.

While I served successive six-day tours at the Golan OPs, my wife Christina (Chris) and our two children, Alexandra (Alex, 10) and Andy (8), found an apartment in Tiberias and explored biblical sites, shopped in local markets, or swam at the YMCA on Lake Tiberias.

In 1972 both parties sporadically violated the cease-fire along the Golan Heights, the Israelis with over-flights and the Palestinian Fatah brigade stationed on the Syrian side by mortar fire across the line. In retaliation for the mortar attacks, the Israeli Air Force bombed military targets along the Syrian side of the Golan or even deeper inside Syria. These activities kept observers alert and reduced the monotony of quiet periods. During those times, we observed Israeli and Syrian activity near their positions. The Syrians had low earth bunkers and long trenches, and they stayed put except for occasional supply runs. The Israelis constantly improved their battle positions by building both a 25-kilometer long anti-tank ditch close to the cease-fire lines and long earth mounds parallel to the ditch and 600 meters in front of it. They positioned tank platoons on reverse slopes well behind the long earth works. Later, during my inspection tours of OPs on the Syrian side, I noticed that none of the Israeli tank platoons behind the long earth mounds were visible from the Syrian side. The Israelis also built stone bunkers for their infantry. In sum, their "preparation of the battlefield" was thorough and systematic.

During April 1972, I did my familiarization at OPs along the Suez Canal. The outposts consisted of a living-observation trailer and a steel reinforced bunker under a large sand mound. To alleviate the heat, each trailer had a second palmetto roof about one foot above the trailer. One of our OPs on the Egyptian side sat atop a large semi-destroyed building in the ghost town of Suez City near where the Suez Canal enters Suez Bay. In 1970 and 1971, heavy exchanges of artillery fire between Egypt and Israel had left the city in ruins, its people evacuated. Beginning in 1967, the Israelis built a 40-to-60-foot tall sand barrier along the entire stretch of the canal, and the Egyptians built even taller mounds that looked like platoon-size shooting platforms on their side. Despite the "preparation of the battlefield" activities by both sides, I do not recall any cease-fire violations along the Suez Canal in April of 1972.

In May 1972, a letter from Lieutenant General Dutch Kerwin, the Army Deputy Chief of Staff for Personnel, "frocked" me to the "apparent" grade (rank without pay or impact on promotion sequence) of lieutenant colonel, and I assumed my duties as COO. Though having learned of "frockings" done earlier in our Army's history, I had heard of none since my commissioning in 1959. As a result, General Kerwin's action came as a surprise. Accepted to serve as the COO while a major, I expected to do the job at that rank. I soon learned that Kerwin intended to counter another country's move to place one of its own lieutenant colonels into the UNTSO COO position. As a result, I prematurely became a lieutenant colonel and assumed the COO duties–the first of many times I was amazed by the amount of politics involved in international organizations.

In Jerusalem Christina and I could not find an apartment in the Israeli part of the city but with the help of another member of UNTSO, Sergeant Major Jack Willard, U.S. Army, we rented an Arab house next to one that he and his wife rented amid olive groves in the town of El Azzaria (named after Biblical Lazarus) and along the road to Jericho just outside the Jerusalem city limits. This house stood across a gravel road near the tomb of Lazarus. Further along that ancient gravel road stood an Orthodox church; a bit higher up the road, a Muslim mosque; and on top of the hill, the ruins of a Crusader castle. Glad to live near Jack and Louise Willard, we also had simple and good Palestinian neighbors whose children played along the ancient road or in the olive groves around our homes. During the school year our children, Andy and Alex, had to take an Arab bus full of people and animals to the center of Jerusalem and then a crowded Israeli bus to the International Anglican Church School deeper into the Israeli part of the city. Needless to say, they enjoyed an extensive exposure to new cultures, and both parents and children gained historical insights into this troubled land.

General Siilasvuo arranged for me to make official visits to our control stations in Damascus and Cairo. While there I also made office calls on the Syrian and Egyptian officials responsible for maintaining liaison with UNTSO. In Syria I called on General Tiara, an intelligence officer and distant relative of President Assad. In Egypt, I met with Colonel Helmi. They both received me cordially and pledged continued support for the UN mission. My visit to Syria proved particularly important: After the 1967 War, Syria and the U.S. broke diplomatic relations, but because of our UN positions, my predecessors as COO and I were the only Americans allowed to visit that country. In Damascus the chief of our control station was a Swedish lieutenant colonel, Sven Svensson, a wounded veteran of the Swedish contingent of volunteers who had served with the Finnish Army along its World War II front against the Soviet Union. In Kantara, an Egyptian town on the western side of the Suez Canal, the chief of our control station was a French Foreign Legion veteran, Commandant Wolloch. Svensson, Wolloch, and their staffs briefed me, and I also visited some of the OPs on their sides of the cease-fire line. The terrain between the Golan Heights and Damascus and the flatlands with occasional dense vegetation between the Suez Canal and Cairo fascinated me.

During my visit to Egypt, I also learned that President Anwar Sadat had asked all Soviet advisors to leave Egypt, which led to an invitation from Colonel Helmi to visit his headquarters in Kantara to participate in celebrations resulting from that development. The Egyptian officers struck me as truly happy that the Russians had departed, and they spoke openly about the humiliations they had suffered from the Soviets.

During 1972, Israel focused mainly on terrorist activity because Islamic terrorists had killed eleven of their athletes during the Munich summer Olympics and Japanese terrorists had executed a bloody attack at Lod Airport near Tel-Aviv. Before those two events, late in May, the Fedayeen in southern Lebanon had made mortar attacks on and raided Israeli settlements. In response, Israeli Defense Forces, for the first time, crossed into southern Lebanon and occupied the area up to the Litani River. A few weeks later, UN resolutions led Israel to withdraw from Lebanon and authorized UNTSO to establish five observation posts on the Lebanese side of the Israeli-Lebanese border.

My first major challenge as COO was making a reconnaissance of the Lebanese border area to select locations for the OPs. With my French Marine deputy, Capitaine-de-Frigate Pierre Campanet, we set out to do what had to be done. Traveling from Nakoura, on the Mediterranean coast, through small Lebanese villages eastward, we selected five OP locations that had reasonable road access and a view of large segments of the border.

We met trouble in only one village. At an intersection in Marjayoun, a roadblock of burning tires and a group of armed militiamen demanded to know our identity. Some of them spoke French, and Pierre Campanet calmly explained who we were and on whose authority we acted. They made some calls on their radio, and after a few anxious hours sitting in our Jeep Wagoneer with weapons pointed at us, we heard more chatter on their radio and they let us pass.

In two or three days, with our selection of OP sites completed, we guided a UNTSO logistic column that would set up the OP equipment at the new sites, some in deserted buildings. At that time UNTSO had a control station in Beirut, Lebanon. The officer in charge (OIC), a French lieutenant colonel, led some twenty observers who would man the newly selected OPs. Using frequency-modulated (FM) radio, reports from the OPs would go directly to UNTSO in Jerusalem and simultaneously, for information, to the control station in Beirut. The control station in Beirut could listen to the OP radio traffic but could not communicate directly with Government House in Jerusalem. The new OPs provided a relayed FM radio link capability with Beirut, an improvement over the unreliable single side band radio link with the Beirut control station.

While we began observer operations on the Lebanese side of the Israel-Lebanon border, the Israelis put up a fence and created a plowed strip of land along their side of that border. By early fall 1972, Fatah or Fedayeen activity in Lebanon subsided, and my attention returned to the other sectors of our responsibility. Along the Suez Canal and on the Golan Heights, all remained quiet. With little happening, our duty hours at Government House ended in mid-afternoon, with the weekends free.

In the fall of 1972 I attended, by invitation, the Damascus funeral of a relative of President Sadat. General Siilasvuo felt it would do no harm for me to attend as an UNTSO official. After my arrival in Damascus, General Tiara called my hotel room to brief me on what to do when I attended the mourning for the deceased on the next day. When we arrived at a large complex of a mosque and surrounding buildings, General Tiara stayed behind while I, wearing the required civilian clothing, was ushered through crowds of mourners in the outer buildings to some inner rooms reserved for family mourners. Alone in a room with satin wall and floor carpets and a few chairs but no other mourners, I received from a Muslim attendant a small cup of strong Turkish coffee. As briefed, I drank the coffee while meditating and mourning the deceased. After ten or fifteen minutes, the attendant brought a second cup of coffee. After another repetition of that process, I could leave.

Shortly after the third cup but before I ended my third ten-minute period of mourning, a neatly dressed gentleman of about sixty entered and extending his hand said: "Welcome, Colonel Krawciw. I am Minister of the Interior Sassa, Class of 1956, Command and General Staff College at Fort Leavenworth, Kansas." He wanted to know information on some American officers whom he had known and specifically asked about General Westmoreland. I told him what I knew: that they were well and where they were. He then told me he had word from "his people" in Palestine that my family and I were good to the people in El Azzaria. He regretted that the U.S. did not have relations with Syria but said that my family and I were always welcome and that we could travel anywhere within Syria without escort. I thanked him, wished him and his family all the best, and left.

I often wondered who in El Azzaria passed the information about me to the Syrians. I came to the conclusion that it must have been our "house boy," Ibrahim, a stocky thirty-year-old Palestinian the mayor of El Azzaria, Khatib, recommended to us. Mayor Khatib later invited us to his home for dinner one evening. During the course of the meal, I asked him why so many children in his town had reddish hair and freckles. He then told me that, while Palestinians descend from ancient Philistines, many other historic cultures had contributed to his people's origin. He then pointed at the ruins of the Crusader castle next to his home and said: "You have to know that an Irish Crusader unit lived here for nearly two hundred years in the Middle Ages. We descend also from them." As for our helper, Ibrahim, we retained him until we departed the area in the spring of 1974. He made frequent weekend trips to stay with his family in Gaza. Undoubtedly a member of some Palestinian organization, he was a good cook and handyman and became a good friend of my family. Minister Sassa's permission for me and my family to travel anywhere in Syria enabled us to see many parts of that country, including the mountainous northeastern portions inhabited by people who spoke Aramaic, the language of Israel during the time of Christ.

Through the wet winter 1972-73, only minor cease-fire violations occurred, and I had a chance to develop new standard operating procedures for observers' reports and the four control stations on the Golan and Suez. Principally, that meant that during periods of heavy military activity across cease-fire lines, the observers would implement controlled sequential reporting, which ensured minimal duplication of reports and kept observers at different OPs from cutting each other off. Since UNTSO lacked an updated evacuation plan for dependents, I developed one similar to that of the U.S. Army, Europe. Based on that plan, UNTSO could, if necessary, evacuate its dependents from Jerusalem and Cairo to British bases in Cyprus and dependents from Jordan and Damascus to Beirut and then to Cyprus if Beirut became unsafe. The plan required extensive coordination with officials of the countries involved and with British and Cypriot authorities.

In the spring and early summer of 1973, incidents on the Golan

Heights grew more frequent. Israeli air strikes quickly followed Syrian or Fatah mortar attacks on Israeli "kibbutzim" (collective farms), a cycle that repeated every few weeks. Along the Suez Canal, the Egyptian Army frantically worked on its high sand mounds – fighting positions that were higher than the Israeli sand wall on the other side of the Canal. The UNTSO Political Advisor, Remy Gorge, a Swiss gentleman, and many diplomats in Jerusalem believed that another Arab-Israeli war would break out by mid-summer. By July or August, however, all the military activities on the Golan and along the Canal ceased. We also learned that the Syrians moved the Fatah brigade away from the cease-fire lines.

In September 1973, an air action over northwestern Syria, in which Israeli fighter jets shot down a large number of Syrian MIGs, shattered the calm. Shortly thereafter, Commandant Walloch from Kantara and Lieutenant Colonel Svensson from Damascus reported large-scale troop movements toward the cease-fire lines. Observers at OPs also reported increased activity along both the Egyptian and Syrian positions.

On September 24, I drove to Damascus to visit Svensson and inspect some OPs. The next day, while I was in Damascus, he and his staff told me of notices around town calling upon bakers to start stocking extra bread, directing doctors to report to military hospitals on 1 October, and announcing cancellation of various bus lines. On my way to the OPs, I noticed a lot of military movement to within 20 kilometers of the cease-fire lines. Much of it appeared to be movement into forward assembly areas.

Upon returning to Jerusalem, I reported what I had seen to General Siilasvuo and Mr. Gorge. Though what I had seen did not constitute cease-fire violations, the UN Secretary General had charged General Siilasvuo to watch for signs of increasing tensions. What I reported clearly fell into that category, and General Siilasvuo concluded that he should travel to Egypt to observe conditions there. Mr. Gorge and I warned him that, if similar activities were going on in Egypt, the Egyptians might not let him return to Jerusalem. He nonetheless decided to go and on 1 October departed by UN executive jet through Cyprus to Cairo. Colonel Bunworth, the UNTSO Senior Staff Officer, had finished his tour of duty and departed for Ireland a few weeks earlier, leaving me—a major frocked to lieutenant colonel—in charge of UNTSO headquarters.

On 3 October we learned that the Egyptians had placed General Siilasvuo under house arrest in Cairo, barring his return to Jerusalem. Two days later, our observers reported more military movement toward the cease-fire lines. That evening, General Moshe Dayan, the Israeli Minister of Defense, called me by phone and asked whether I had contact with UNTSO's control station in Damascus. Upon learning that I did, he asked that I pass through UNTSO's offices in Damascus a message from him to the Syrian authorities. The message stated that Israel has no hostile intentions. As the situation worsened, I feared that Israel's Yom Kippur (Day of Atonement), a most solemn holy day only hours away, might become "another Tet" (remembering the 1968 Tet offensive in Vietnam). On Yom Kippur, Jews may not listen to the radio or watch television. If war broke out during the holiday, public announcements would go unheard.

On the morning of Saturday, 6 October, loudspeaker trucks on Jerusalem streets told people of a general mobilization. The OPs, however, sent no reports of military activities. That remained so until 2:00 p.m., when "all hell broke loose" simultaneously along the Suez Canal and on the Golan Heights. UNTSO's radios came alive with hundreds of reports, and I had to impose the controlled net procedures developed earlier. OPs on both cease-fire lines reported heavy Egyptian and Syrian air strikes and artillery fire on Israeli positions along the Suez

115

Canal and on the Golan Heights. Simultaneously, Egyptian combat engineers began constructing eleven bridges along the Suez Canal, while sappers on rafts with high-pressure water cannons started to wash down the Israeli sand wall at locations where the bridges would reach the Israeli side of the Canal. At the same time, the OPs reported Syrian tank divisions crossing the cease-fire lines.

As the battle progressed, the OPs continued to report. Egyptian engineers completed the bridges and broke through the sand wall in about eight hours, much faster than prewar Israeli estimates. As Egyptian armor moved across the canal, their infantry fanned out and overpowered most of the Israeli infantry's strong points. The Israeli Air Force attempted to knock out the eleven bridges in continuous air strikes but destroyed only one while losing some fifty of its aircraft to Egyptian surface-to-air missiles (SAM-6s). Slowed by the lack of public attention to radios and TVs on Yom Kippur, Israel's mobilization failed to assemble its armor and infantry counterattack forces until late on 7 October. Artillery and support units took even longer to join the fight.

Fortunately for Israel, Minister Dayan had moved the famous 7th Armored (Golani) Brigade from rest and re-fitting back to the Golan a few days earlier when Israeli intelligence had picked up some of the Syrian movements at about the same time that I noticed them on 25 and 26 September. I later learned that despite that reinforcement, the Israeli government had not wanted to do more so as not to provoke Syria into hostilities. The Israelis believed that Syria had no intention to initiate war. The Golani brigade broke up the three-division Syrian main attack near Kuneitra and northward. Skillful use of the prepared battle area and hastily formed small unit strike-force counterattacks took a heavy toll of the attackers over the next two nights and days. Though left with only six operational tanks by 9 October, the 7th Armored Brigade held its ground.

In the southern sector of the Golan Heights, Syrian air strikes and artillery barrages destroyed the Barak Brigade's headquarters and killed its commander, and Israeli close-air support proved ineffective due to an extensive and mobile Syrian air-defense umbrella. Our observers reported many Israeli aircraft shot down. Protected from air attacks, two Syrian brigades broke through in that sector. After gaining some ground, however, they slowed their advance and failed to dash for their objectives, the bridges spanning the Jordan River.

Meanwhile, a tank battalion from one of the Syrian main attack divisions nearly overran the Israeli command post some 10 kilometers southwest of Kuneitra. Syrian tanks knocked out seven of the ten Centurion tanks in the security force of the Israeli headquarters, and its staff began destroying documents. The tank battalion did not stop to secure the overrun command post but moved on to the east toward the Jordan River, a fact I learned after the war from Israeli Brigadier General Uri Baron, the deputy commander of the Golan Heights front. (Back in 1963-64, Lieutenant Colonel Uri Baron had been my classmate at the Armor Officers Career Course at Fort Knox. I saw the destroyed Centurions some days later while attempting to reach some of our OPs near Kuneitra to remove trapped observers from the battle area.) While all this happened, observers continued to report all activities near the Canal and on the Golan. We lost contact with a few OPs, and the remainder reported heavy damage to their vehicles and living trailers.

The Fatah brigade that had been in Syria suddenly reappeared in southern Lebanon, and UNTSO OPs along the Lebanese border reported exchanges of artillery, mortar, and small arms fire along their line. One team of UN observers found themselves caught in the midst of a nighttime firefight between Fatah and Israeli infantry. When the Fatah fighters edged closer to the OP, the two observers hid in a disposal pit. Though Fatah fighters occupied the OP premises and used it as a fighting position for most of that night, they withdrew in the morning.

Once across the Canal, Egyptian armor preceded by infantry moved some ten kilometers into the Sinai desert and set up a defensive line that consisted of infantry dug in with Sagger anti-tank missiles positioned some three thousand meters in front of their line of tanks. When the Israelis mounted a hasty counterattack on 8 October, the Saggers decimated the brigade before it could engage Egyptian armor. Watching TV at Government House, we saw the Egyptians parade the captured brigade commander and many of his men through Cairo's streets.

Within the Israeli Southern Command, in-fighting occurred between Major General Ariel Sharon, who as a division commander wanted to press hasty counterattacks, and General Shmuel Gonnen, his superior, who warned that artillery to suppress Egyptian infantry was not ready to support such attacks. Sharon had retired as the Sinai commander in the summer of 1973. One of his division commanders, Gonnen, had assumed command of the front. After the 6 October mobilization, the Israelis reactivated Sharon and sent him to the Sinai as a division commander. With their roles now reversed, Sharon became so insubordinate that many of the Israeli officers talked openly about this friction. Prime Minister Golda Meir and Defense Minister Moshe Dayan had to referee between the squabbling generals.

On the northern front, the Syrian line remained under the SAM-6 umbrella. After a shaky mobilization start on 6-7 October, the Israelis attempted to organize a defense and launch a counterattack from the Jordan River toward the base of the Golan Heights. Generals Rafael Eitan, the commander of the Golan front, and Uri Baron, his deputy, after stopping the Syrian attack on 8 October, commenced a three-division assault to regain ground in the direction of the partially surrounded Golani Brigade, which still held its positions near the old cease-fire lines.

At Government House and at all UNTSO's control stations, the small operations staff worked around the clock to stay in touch with our OPs and forward reports of combat activity. My staff consisted of three operations officers: Capitaine-de-Frigate Pierre Campanet, my French deputy; Major Alan Windsor, Australian Army; and Captain Helmut Jankowy, Austrian Army. Sergeant Major Jack Willard assisted us whenever he could break away from his other duties. All five of us slept very little during the first four nights of the war. On 10 October the Egyptians released General Siilasvuo, and he returned to Jerusalem. We were, of course, delighted to see him. Many decisions had to be made, the first being to discontinue OP reporting. With all-out war underway, it made no sense to report cease-fire violations. We nevertheless needed to stay in touch with the OPs in order to plan for their relief or re-supply until they could be evacuated. Most of them had reported the destruction of their vehicles and living trailers, and Government House had lost contact with a number of OPs in heavy combat areas. Our worst fears were that some of UNTSO's personnel might be dead or wounded.

On 11 October General Siilasvuo and I drove to the Tiberias control station for a briefing by its officer in charge, Lieutenant Colonel Keith Howard, Australian Army. Looking across Lake Tiberias from the control station, we could see that a blanket of dense smoke from the on-going battle clouded the Golan Heights. Colonel Howard told us that he had no contact with two or three OPs but that personnel of the others, though without food, remained in their bunkers. Due for relief on 6 October, observers at half of his OPs had already consumed most of their food and water by that date. The outbreak of the war prevented both relief and re-supply. A similar situation prevailed on the Syrian side of the line and along the Suez Canal.

A few days earlier Colonel Howard organized observer relief teams that tried to follow the Israeli counterattack but Israeli military police

119

turned them around due to intense meeting engagements just ahead between Israeli and Syrian tank units that, due to thick smoke, had collided within a few hundred yards of each other. Howard planned to try again after the Israelis regained the old cease-fire lines.

We did have one successful UN operation following a tragic Israeli bombing raid on Damascus. In an effort to knock out the Syrian Air Force headquarters, the Israeli pilots, dodging barrages of SAM-6s, missed their target and destroyed many homes in the nearby suburbs. A number of diplomatic families lost their lives, and UNTSO lost a Norwegian observer and his family. Following that incident, UNTSO decided to evacuate its dependents from Damascus to Beirut, as planned a year earlier. During the evacuation, Israel declared that it would not attack the Damascus-Beirut highway and, with Syrian military escort, some two hundred members of UNTSO and Diplomatic Corps families left the Syrian war zone for Lebanon. Families in Jerusalem and Cairo prepared for evacuation to Cyprus if war activities reached those cities. I had a chance to stop at home in El Azzaria some time in the middle of the war and found Christina packed and ready to move. Alex and Andy were excited by all the activity. They, too, were ready.

Between 12 and 14 October, the Israelis did more than regain the old lines. They penetrated some 30 kilometers deeper into Syria along the Kuneitra-Damascus road and beat back an attack by an Iraqi division that arrived to reinforce the Syrians. At that point, the Israeli cabinet decided to revert to the defensive on the Golan Heights and shift its best units, which had made the counterattack, to the Sinai. In an amazing feat of mobility along interior lines, they accomplished that in two days. Hundreds of tank transporters loaded with anti-tank mines moved to the new defensive line on the Golan, unloaded their mines for use in setting up protective minefields, and then loaded the tanks and headed for the Sinai. That enabled the Israeli command in the Sinai to organize a well-planned counterattack, with the support of artillery and infantry, to dispose of Sagger teams. That attack, led by Adan's and Sharon's divisions, penetrated the Egyptian defenses between the Egyptian Second and Third Armies near Ismalia on the night of 16 October near an area known as the Chinese Farm. This Israeli attack also gained a bridge crossing over the Canal and secured a bridgehead on its western side.

During the next few days, General Sharon's division tried to cross a 40-meter-wide canal that ran from the Suez Canal just north of Ismalia toward Cairo. He aimed to get behind the Egyptian Second Army. Egyptian infantry and armor on the other side of what we called "the Sweet Water Canal" repelled all Sharon's attempts. On 18 October, Minister Dayan, who personally came to see what stalled the Israeli offensive, made a decision to quit trying to flank the Egyptian Second Army and, instead, to shift forces to the south toward the city of Suez and surround the Egyptian Third Army. That task fell to General Avraham Adan's division in the southern portion of the Israeli bridgehead.

By that time, all belligerents had begun receiving a lot of international pressure to cease hostilities. On 19 October, UNTSO received a warning order to prepare for a new cease-fire. That entailed marking the forward positions and mine fields of the belligerents, reporting cease-fire violations, and helping locate missing and dead Egyptian, Israeli, and Syrian soldiers. In the international political arena, Henry Kissinger embarked on a shuttle mission between Jerusalem, Cairo, and Damascus.

Also on 19 October, I drove to our Sinai control station, some 20 kilometers east of the Canal, to inform our Finnish officer in charge there of his new mission after a cease-fire and to inspect the damage caused by two Egyptian air strikes. Based on the extensive damage at all our OPs, it appeared that the Egyptian and Syrian governments had never briefed their ground and air combat units on the location of UNTSO positions. I also confirmed that since the first few hours of the war, the Sinai control station had had no contact with two observers at an OP near an Israeli position on the Suez Canal. The officer in charge and I agreed to organize a search for the missing observers as soon as possible after the cease-fire, which required obtaining the help of the Egyptian army that still held the area near the missing observers' OP.

After a day in Jerusalem, I left again on 21 October to meet with Keith Howard in Tiberias and proceed with him to the Golan Heights to bring back observers still stranded at various OPs on both sides of the old cease-fire lines. When we arrived at an OP manned by U.S. Navy Lieutenant Commander Al Waugaman and a Dutch officer, we found all their equipment destroyed and both observers caring for nearly thirty wounded Syrian soldiers within their OP compound, which then only consisted of a three-foot-high stone wall. An Israeli lieutenant who spoke English walked down from the nearby position of his tank platoon and told us that, as the tank battle raged around them, the two observers time and again left their bunker to pull wounded Syrian soldiers from damaged or burning tanks. I asked the Israeli lieutenant to write out statements about the deeds of the two observers. He said he would gladly do it and obtain more such statements from other officers and NCOs in his unit. From the OP, I counted more than 80 destroyed Syrian tanks.

Al Waugaman told Keith Howard and me that the Israeli tank platoon near his OP would stay 300 to 400 meters on the reverse slope behind one of the long berms mentioned before. Then, as Syrian tank formations came within a few hundred yards, the Israeli tanks would appear near the earth mound and engage targets, only to move quickly back and then reappear at another location near the berm and engage more targets. With Al Waugaman and his partner in our jeeps, we proceeded north through Kuneitra and along the long anti-tank ditch to reach other OPs. Along the anti-tank ditch, we saw dozens of Syrian tanks, armored personnel carriers, and bridge carriers knocked out or stuck in the obstacle. While picking up other observers, Keith Howard and I counted more than three hundred destroyed or abandoned vehicles within sight of the road we traveled. We could also see evidence of the Israelis' assault to retake the high position on Mount Hermon they had lost to a daring Syrian raid on the first day of the war.

Following the war, I forwarded to USN headquarters a recommendation for a Navy Cross for Lieutenant Commander Al Waugaman in recognition of his heroism on the Golan Heights. Since UNTSO observers were noncombatants, the Navy downgraded the award to a Legion of Merit.

We also wanted to bring back two observers trapped behind minefields on the Syrian side of the old cease-fire lines southeast of Kuneitra. Behind them was a line of Centurion tanks belonging to the Jordan Legion. They had entered Syria as a good will gesture toward their Arab brethren but did not seek heavy combat with the Israelis. Periodically they lobbed a few ineffective shells towards the Israeli positions, and the Israelis politely sent a few shots toward the Jordanians. Before we could remove the observers from the OP in front of the Jordanian brigade, we had to get a local cease-fire from both sides, which we obtained the next day. The two observers walked two kilometers towards us while we waited for them at Al Waugaman's destroyed OP. They had been out of food for about ten days and, to survive, ended up eating their cat. Both had lost a lot of weight but were happy to be alive.

Between 19 and 21 October, General Adan's division attacked to the south along flat lands on the western side of the Canal toward the city of Suez. Eight to ten kilometers north of that city, the terrain became heavily vegetated, and Egyptian defenders stopped the Israeli advance. General Adan then moved some of his forces southwest to the Suez-Cairo road and began to prepare for an attack on the city along that road. On that day, 22 October, the UN Security Council passed a cease-fire resolution that the Israeli government accepted. UNTSO thereupon ordered Commandant Wolloch to dispatch a group of observer teams to General Adan's headquarters to inform him that, based on the cease-fire accepted by Egypt and Israel, UNTSO needed to start marking the forward positions of his units. Adan told the senior observer in that group that he "was not finished doing what he was doing" and that our observers should "get out of his way." The observer teams reported what had happened and moved about a mile away to observe his next moves.

In late afternoon of 22 October, General Adan commenced an attack on Suez from the west, along the main road from Cairo. An armor-infantry task force, without air or artillery support, dashed into the outskirts of the city, where it endured almost complete destruction by Egyptian infantry armed with rocket propelled grenade launchers firing down on the column from upper level windows and rooftops. Though a few tanks broke through to the center of the city, most of the task force's vehicles burned in the outskirts. Dead and wounded Israelis littered the street. Shortly after that debacle, General Adan called for our observers to help remove his dead and wounded. As Commandant Wolloch still had a few observers in Suez, he got in touch with them and the Red Cross in Cairo asking all of them to proceed to where the battle had occurred. He also asked the Israelis and the Egyptians to ensure safe passage for the Red Cross and UNTSO observer teams. When these teams arrived at the scene, the Egyptians prevented removal of Israeli casualties until news media began photographing the gory sights. Finally, the next morning, the teams removed the casualties.

Hostilities did not end until the night of 23 October when, unable to reach Suez Bay through the city, the Israeli High Command decided to capture the high escarpment southwest of Suez that abutted Suez Bay. That night an Israeli airborne brigade secured those heights. With that action, Israeli forces surrounded the Egyptian Third Army and could prevent supplies reaching it from Cairo.

Syria also accepted the cease-fire on 23 October. UNTSO then began its new mission to mark the forward positions of belligerents, search for their missing in action, and report the sporadic exchanges of fire that continued until the signature of disengagement agreements on 18 January 1974, along the Suez, and 31 May 1974, on the Golan Heights.

With Egyptian help we found the two missing observers (one French and one Italian) in a shallow grave near their OP, probably killed by Egyptian assault units on the first day of the war. UNTSO also obtained the release of a number of its observers mistakenly taken by Syrian units on the Golan Heights. One of them was Captain John Holly, USMC. The Syrians had marched him barefoot with other prisoners to Damascus. Once the Syrians confirmed that he was not an Israeli soldier, they put him in a hospital to treat his lacerated feet. Some days before his return through Lebanon, President Assad visited him to apologize for the error by his troops. Overall, UNTSO was fortunate in not having more casualties than it did during that short but very intense war.

Early in November the Army recalled me to Washington for a week to brief General Abrams, the Army Chief of Staff, and other Army Staff officers on what I had observed during the war. When I walked into General Abrams' office, the first thing he asked was whether observer so-and-so had gotten his equipment replaced. Not knowing what had happened, I was a bit stunned. He realized that and told me there had been an artillery exchange on the Golan Heights while I was traveling and one of our U.S. observers lost all the field equipment in the living trailer of his OP. Both observers on that OP had dashed for their bunker and escaped unhurt. I was amazed that the Army Operations Center passed this type of detail, based on UN reports, to the Army Chief of Staff. His response did, however, demonstrate his concern for the care of our soldiers. General Abrams showed great interest in the many impressions that I have recounted in this story. Before the end of the week, I also briefed a large group of Foreign Service officers at the State Department.

Before I had left for Washington at the end of October, General Siilasvuo set up a meeting between Egyptian General Muhammad al Ghani al Gamasy and Israeli General Aharon Yariv at a tent that UNTSO observers put up along Kilometer 101 on the Cairo-Suez road. Disengagement negotiations began. General Yariv demanded that both Egyptian armies pull back west of the Canal while General Gamasy maintained that Egyptian forces would stay along a line some 10 kilometers east of the Canal that they gained during the first days of the war. According to General Siilasvuo, during this first and during all later meetings at Kilometer 101, General Yariv appeared under pressure and kept calling Minister Dayan for negotiation options. General Gamasy, on the other hand, stayed calm, maintained the same position throughout the negotiations, and never called back for instructions. The Israelis hoped to use the surrounded Third Army and its possible demise due to lack of supplies as a negotiation chip, but that backfired. Under international pressure, Israel had to allow food, water, and medical supplies to reach the surrounded army.

Meanwhile, as weeks dragged on, the Israeli economy started suffering because much of its workforce remained mobilized in the many brigades needed to maintain the line along the Canal and in the "bulge" they created between Ismalia and Suez. In the end on 18 January 1974, Israel agreed to the initial demands of Egypt and to the positioning of a UN Emergency Force (UNEF) along a 10-kilometer wide strip between Egyptian and Israeli forces. That meant that the Israeli forward line would be 20 kilometers east of the Suez Canal.

In addition to its other missions, UNTSO was tasked to facilitate the positioning of UNEF. Before that, in November 1973, UNTSO received a reinforcement of 28 American observers (bringing our total to the maximum of 36) and 36 observers from the Soviet Union—the first Soviet participation in a UN peacekeeping mission. Among the new US observers were two colonels and a West Point classmate, Major Tim Plummer. Because the United States had assigned these observers on a temporary duty basis, their wives could not accompany them. One of the senior U.S. officers, Colonel Dashle, remained only a short time. The other senior officer, Colonel Robert Clarke, a friend from a Pentagon assignment, took over my Senior U.S. Military Observer duties.

The senior Soviet observer was an infantry officer, Colonel Bilyk from Kaniv, Ukraine. Because Ukranians constitute about 25% of Soviet combat arms officers, he was stunned to find a Ukranian serving in the U.S. armed forces. He and half his observers assigned to our control station in Kantara, Egypt, found apartments in Cairo and lived there in pairs. The other half of his observers went to Damascus. Colonel Bilyk spoke only Russian and Ukrainian, but all his observers, though they wore infantry, armor or artillery insignia, spoke fluent Arabic, and a few spoke English as well. I had no doubt that most of them, except Colonel Bilyk, were intelligence officers. During one of my visits to Kantara in December 1973, Colonel Bilyk somehow became separated from the Soviet major always found at his side and joined me and Colonel Clarke in our jeep. Alone on the road to Port Said, he said: "Oh, it's so good to be rid of that SOB!"

In November and December 1973, UNEF battalions staged into the

Sinai and base camps in Egypt. They began locating and clearing huge minefields left behind by both Egyptians and Israelis. The President of Finland promoted General Siilasvuo to lieutenant general, and the UN Secretary General bestowed on him the position of UN Assistant Secretary General overseeing both UNTSO and UNEF operations. Recalled from Ireland, Colonel Bunworth took over as acting Chief of Staff of UNTSO, and Keith Howard, promoted to colonel, became UNTSO's Senior Staff Officer. He had been in UNTSO since the 1967 Arab-Israeli War and had been wounded in that conflict as Jordanian forces attacked Jerusalem.

In mid-April my family and I said goodbye to our friends in UNTSO and started our trip by car through Jordan, Syria, Turkey, Greece, Italy, and Austria to Bayreuth in West Germany, where I assumed command of the 1st Squadron, 2nd Armored Cavalry Regiment along another frontier, the border with East Germany and Czechoslovakia. My real promotion to lieutenant colonel came through while on the road from Brindisi to Venice in Italy.

Note: Many of the impressions recorded in this account are based on events and dates as I remember them, hence the possibility of some errors in dates or names. Other information in the story derives from the shared experience and observations of the following friends or colleagues: Lieutenant General Ensio Siilasvuo, Finnish Army; Mr. Remy Gorge, Switzerland; Colonel Bunworth, Irish Army; Brigadier General Uri Baron, IDF; Colonel Keith Howard, Australian Army; Major Tim Plummer, U.S Army; Capitaine Pierre Campanet, French Marine Corps; Major Alan Windsor, Australian Army; Lieutenant Colonel Sven Svensson, Swedish Army; Commandant Wolloch, French Foreign Legion; Captain Youni Kerauvori, U.S. Army (a U.S. observer in Lebanon); Captain John Holly, USMC; Lieutenant Commander Al Waugaman, U.S. Navy; Colonel Helmi, Egyptian Army; and Colonel Bilyk, Soviet Army.

Your Courage to Act with Integrity May have a Major Impact - On You!

by Major General William A. Cohen, USAFR (Ret.)

A young major attending Air Command and Staff School called me while I was on active duty as a senior officer. For a research project, he intended to interview as many serving Air Force general officers as possible in hopes of uncovering common factors leading to their promotion to senior ranks or situations they avoided that might have hindered their advancement.

Though his questions caused me to do some self-analysis, they also provided a good deal of amusement. My career path had hardly been smooth, certainly not one I could recommend to others. My record as a cadet fell well short of sterling. Not since George Armstrong Custer, last man in the Class of 1861, had anyone with a math average lower than mine managed to graduate without first successfully completing a "turnout" examination. I had nevertheless done well in the Air Force, which promoted me to major in 1965, six years after graduation.

Though warned that transferring from B52s to A26s, the aircraft of the Air Commandos, now part of Special Operations, would harm my chances of promotion to the senior ranks, I applied anyway. Not only that, in 1970 I resigned my regular U.S. Air Force commission, turned down a reserve commission, and immigrated to my wife's country

Captain William A. Cohen, 609th Air Command Squadron, 1968.

of birth, Israel. I accepted a commission as a major in the Israeli Air Force reserve and flew combat missions in the Yom Kippur War of 1973.

Back in the U. S. at the age of 41, I sought to regain my Air Force commission, no easy task. I was lucky. Even though my old squadron commander, now Lieutenant General Oliver Lewis, helped me, it still took eighteen months, and I rejoined the Air Force as a captain rather than a major. At the time, promotion to major in the Air Force Reserve required fourteen years commissioned service; I had only eleven at the time of my resignation. Once a very young major, I had become a very old captain with a most unusual service record – no one's pick to become a senior officer. I thought if I could just be promoted to major again, that would satisfy me even if I received no further promotions.

How then do I account for my eventual selection as a senior officer? I think one incident made the difference, and it occurred not in combat as an Air Commando in Vietnam or as a major in the Israeli Air Force. I had previously written about that moment of truth that shaped my professional character and my career but had preferred until now to conceal my identity in the incident. I chose to use the *nom de guerre* "Herb." In reality, I was Herb – and here is Herb's story.

As a young Air Force lieutenant in 1960, Herb was a new navigator on a B52 aircrew. His responsibilities included the programming and launch of air-to-ground cruise missiles called Hound Dogs. Cutting-edge technology at the time, the missiles had all the bugs normally found in newly fielded systems. Aircrews training with the new cruise missile had consequently achieved mixed results. Sometimes the missiles hit their targets. More often they did not even come close.

Because of the missiles' expense, millions of dollars each, the aircrews didn't launch them during training. The crew programmed a simulated launch and was evaluated on a simulated missile strike.

As in an actual launch, the navigator programmed the missiles while they were flying to the launch point. That took several hours, during which Herb updated the missile repeatedly and told its computers the aircraft's location. About thirty minutes from the target, the navigator put the missile into "simulated launch" mode. The missiles themselves then took over the navigation problem and relayed information to the pilots' consoles. Herb instructed the pilots to follow a special needle indicator on their consoles. If the needle turned right, the pilots turned the aircraft right. If the needle turned left, they turned the aircraft left. When they did this, the aircraft followed the course to the target according to information in the missile's computer guidance system. As if they had actually been launched, the airplane followed the same course the missiles would fly.

Fifteen seconds from the target the navigator turned on a tone signal that was broadcast over the radio. On the ground, a Ground Control Intercept (GCI) site tracked Herb's aircraft on radar. At the point where the missile would normally dive into its target, it would automatically terminate Herb's tone signal. The missile's ballistics determined the course it would take to the ground once it started its final dive. Based on the aircraft's radar track and the missile's ballistics, the GCI site calculated where the missile would impact if actually launched. The calculation's accuracy depended on the accuracy of the information that Herb gave the missile's computers during the two hours of updating and programming.

This procedure also permitted the aircrews to make practice bomb runs without actually launching any bombs. The only difference with a simulated bombing was that the pilots followed a needle wired to the bombardier's bombsight instead of the missile's guidance system.

These practice runs had a major impact on the crews' careers. Crews that received good scores gained promotion. Those that did not were held back, and the results were reflected all the way up the chain of command. Woe to a unit commander whose crews got a "bad bomb" or a "bad missile," one that missed the target based upon the data recorded.

Herb's crewmates were far more experienced than he. His aircraft commander, a lieutenant colonel, had been a first sergeant before going to flight school during World War II. At six feet two inches and still big and tough, he looked the part of a top sergeant. His co-pilot was a captain, as was the electronic warfare officer. The senior navigator and bombardier, another veteran of World War II, was also a lieutenant colonel. Finally, the crew had one non-commissioned officer — the tail gunner — who was a master sergeant and Korean War veteran. A lieutenant fresh out of flying school, Herb had never seen combat or previously served in an aircrew.

Herb's crew had made several training flights with missiles. Sometimes they had received credit for target hits, but usually they had not. They were not alone. Many aircrews had similar experiences with the new weapon system. During their initial six months of fielding and training, the aircrews learned to work with the missiles without any penalty for missiles that malfunctioned or missed the target. Missed targets didn't count. When the Air Force later looked for the reason so many air crews had missed their targets, it learned that the missiles' computer and navigational guidance systems were much more sensitive than previously thought. What had initially appeared as poor performance on the part of air crews in fact resulted from errors on the part of the ground crews that maintained and serviced the missiles.

After completion of six months' training on the missile system, Herb's aircraft commander called the crew together. "When we fly our first training mission after alert, we have missiles that will actually be graded for the first time," he said. "We're not going to debate this. We're going to cheat to make sure we get good scores. All I want to know from the navigators is how we're going to do this."

Herb was shocked and speechless. *(Editorial comment: As a West Point cadet, Herb had been taught not to lie, cheat, or steal, or tolerate anyone who does. He observed classmates who made an error in judgment resulting in a false statement. Recognizing the error later, the individuals reported their false statement. In those days there was only one punishment for an honor violation: separation from the Military Academy. These individuals terminated their own careers for the ideal of honor and integrity. This was expected. Honor was considered more important than success, and no compromise was permitted.)*

The senior navigator and bombardier spoke up. "That's easy," he told the aircraft commander. "Don't follow the missile needle. I'll figure out an adjustment for the ballistics, and I'll "bomb" the target using my bombsight. All you have to do is follow the bombsight's needle as we normally do. The tone is the same for the bombsight or the missile. The GCI site will not know that we're actually bombing the target. It will be simple, and no one will know."

Shortly afterwards, Herb's crew was released after a week on alert with their aircraft loaded with nuclear weapons as part of the deterrent against a potential Soviet attack. They had three days of crew rest before getting together to plan the training mission that involved a twelve-hour flight using the guided missiles. The mission would include the simulated missile launch, some regular bomb runs, some navigation and bomb runs at low level, an aerial refueling, and a celestial navigation evaluation.

For Herb those were three days of absolute hell. He had heard rumors of widespread cheating. Now he had received orders to cheat on an evaluation of missiles for which he was responsible. He talked with friends and more experienced officers concerning his crisis of conscience. They told him not to rock the boat. They told Herb to regard this sort of thing as routine and that everybody cheated occasionally. They said that if he did not cheat, it would be the end of his career.

Herb had worked long and hard for his career. His efforts began with earning an appointment to a service academy, from which he had managed to graduate after four difficult years of rigorous schooling. Then, he had spent a year in navigation school and six months in bombardier school, attended Air Force survival training, and completed several weeks of B-52 ground and air training – six years altogether. How could he refuse to cheat and forfeit all he had worked so hard to achieve? "I had been taught integrity," said Herb. "I was taught 'integrity first,' that this was the essential of being an officer. Cheating was contrary to fundamental values that I had been taught and believed in."

When Herb's crew met to plan the mission, he asked to speak to his aircraft commander privately. When alone Herb told him: "If you want to cheat on these missiles, that's up to you, but get yourself a new navigator, because I'm not going to do it." Herb's commander furiously berated him for quite a long time. He then left the room, slamming the door behind him. Scared, Herb thought his career ended. His tough, combat-experienced lieutenant colonel couldn't believe that this young lieutenant had refused a direct order, though hardly a legal one. Literally shaking in his boots, Herb thought his career at an end before it had barely begun. Moreover, his training had not equipped him to pursue another career in order to support his family. The airlines had stopped using navigators, so even this wasn't an option.

An hour or so later, Herb's commander, still angry, said he wanted to see Herb. Alone he told Herb: "Okay. We'll do it your way. But those missiles better be reliable." Herb answered, "I'll do everything possible to make them so, but I won't cheat." He heard later that his commander had remarked, "I don't know whether Herb's a good navigator or not, but I trust him. He's honest and he's got guts."

The missiles – or was it the ground crew – proved reliable. To this day Herb doesn't know if he was skilled or simply lucky. But here's something Herb did know. He knew how far he would go for what he believed to be right. His answer was all the way.

Herb later became a general. "I believe," he wrote, "that overcoming that personal crisis helped me immensely over the years, and I believe that I owe whatever success I achieved, in part, to it. In fact, it still affects my thinking. Had it ended my career then and there, it still would have been worth it for this priceless piece of knowledge about me."

That's Herb's story. It is also my story. At the time, the crisis was the worse thing that had happened to me. Though I later flew in combat in Vietnam and the Middle East, nothing I ever did was as hard as refusing to obey a direct order to cheat regardless of the personal consequences.

What does this mean to cadets and officer candidates studying to earn a commission? I've heard that "it's a jungle out there" and that you have to do unethical things because of competition in the marketplace, or because you owe it to your family, or whatever. I once interviewed the CEO of a major corporation who resigned from top management jobs with two major corporations, one after the other, over ethical issues. He had both a wife and two young children. So honor and integrity are not just words, not just for the military, and they don't just end at graduation.

I am not suggesting that lieutenants should go looking for trouble. Before cheating, however, they might ask themselves how many battles, companies, campaigns, and even countries and lives would have been saved and been so much better if individuals had maintained integrity and put their honor first. And just maybe their act of integrity will not only benefit others but themselves as well. It did me.

Surviving a Bad Command

by Colonel Andrew P. O'Meara, Jr., USA (Ret.)

Great leaders tell us by their example that there is no such thing as a bad command. Despite scanty clothing, drafty log cabins to protect men from freezing conditions, and meager rations for his soldiers at Valley Force, George Washington never would have labeled the Continental Army a bad command. Nor would Douglas McArthur have tarnished the dignity of his men by claims he had led a bad command at Corregidor, despite the Imperial Japanese Army attacks that defeated the last American resistance on the Bataan Peninsula during the opening campaign by the Americans in World War II. Nor would George Armstrong Custer have described his as a bad command before braves and squaws scalped the last of the fallen soldiers of the 7th Cavalry at the Battle of the Little Big Horn.

For Washington and McArthur, great leadership and an indomitable spirit made possible American victories over determined opponents, while poor intelligence and poor planning allowed victory to elude Custer and the men of the 7th Cavalry. The point is that not all commanders are dealt a winning hand. Each commander must play the hand dealt by fate to his or her command. The hard truth is that few leaders can be called truly great commanders, and some commanders have bad experiences in commands that fall upon hard times, as did Custer and the men of the 7th Cavalry. Discussion of lessons learned in hard times helps to fortify the spirit when warriors come face to face with unpleasant realities. The following essay describes what happened when American troop units experienced hard times imposed by austere budgets during the Vietnam War.

Once a powerful and respected field force, Seventh Army became a bad command during the Vietnam War. I served there before, during and after that bitter war, and I experienced the decline of the once proud command.

In *The 25-Year War* General Bruce Palmer concluded that decisions made by the Department of Defense (DOD) rendered that "once magnificent American field Army...incapable" of performing its important mission of defending NATO.[1] With regret, he acknowledged that the once mighty army had become a replacement training activity in support of the war in Vietnam. General Palmer's conclusions are accurate, but they don't tell the whole story.

In addition to draftees, Seventh Army's replacements consisted of second lieutenants in lieu of captains and junior sergeants to fill the vacancies created by the transfer of senior non-commissioned officers to units preparing for deployment to South Vietnam. Inadequate manning levels were not a temporary measure; they became a crutch for the Department of Defense (DOD) to make ends meet during the long war in Vietnam. The cutbacks in manpower remained in force from 1964 until the end of American participation in the war. A drastic reduction in supplies in the pipeline to sustain training and maintenance operations accompanied the drain of qualified leaders. The results were predictable. Seventh Army went into a decline documented in harsh terms by "indicators of indiscipline" – racial incidents and escalating crime rates.[2]

My memory of the period includes tanks not combat ready, as well as poorly trained and dispirited tank crews. Willing young leaders lacked the qualifications to train their units. Demoralized troops lived in long neglected barracks where the stink of raw sewage seeped through rotted plumbing to haunt the living both day and night. The Vietnam War was a bad time to be a soldier in Seventh Army.

Shortly before he died, General Harold K. Johnson confessed his deep regrets over his failure to resign in protest when the Secretary of Defense

---

[1] General Bruce Palmer, Jr., *The Twenty-five Year War: America's Military Role in Vietnam* (Lexington: University Press of Kentucky, 1984), 175

[2] Guenter Lewy, *America in Vietnam* (New York: Oxford University Press, 1978), 127-61.

(SECDEF) forced the Army Chief of Staff to adopt austerity measures that gutted the Army serving in Europe and in the Continental United States (CONUS) during the Vietnam War.[3] The SECDEF, Robert S. McNamara, imposed stringent reductions in manpower and maintenance support to pay for the Vietnam War. He demanded that the services do more with less, and he diverted to the war resources needed to pay for combat readiness. Exacerbating the problem, the SECDEF insisted that determined leadership maintain combat readiness at the unit level. That created a dilemma for commanders, who nevertheless saw the readiness of their units steadily decline. The contradiction between stated objectives and resources required to pay for combat readiness created a paradox – the McNamara Paradox – the assignment of missions without the personnel and the resources to pay for unit training and maintenance operations.

Operating under severe handicaps, the senior leadership of DOD sacrificed Army units in NATO and the United States to pay for an undeclared war. The SECDEF had told the Congress that the operations in Vietnam were limited in nature, and President Lyndon Johnson ran for re-election on a peace platform in the fall of 1964. In the absence of a candid DOD accounting for the war's costs, Congress failed to provide the resources required for sustained combat operations of the expanded military forces in Vietnam. The SECDEF made up the difference by diverting from the training base and units manning the frontiers of freedom the troops, leaders, supplies, and equipment needed to fight the war in Vietnam.[4]

The troop units of Seventh Army guarding the NATO frontier soon fell upon hard times as the flow of replacements and repair parts for them dried up. The senior leadership told commanders to maintain combat ready units without adequate fuel, ammunition, repair parts, and replacements

---

[3] H.R. McMaster, *Dereliction of Duty: Lyndon Johnson, Robert McNamara, the Joint Chiefs of Staff, and the Lies that Led to Vietnam* (New York: Harper Collins, 1998), 318.
[4] *Ibid.*, 323-334.

to achieve combat readiness. Many commanders at all levels predictably observed Army Regulations in the breach. Some commanders held the line, accurately reporting the status of their units; they were relieved of command. Others gave an appearance of following orders to make do with less by cutting corners and putting the best face possible on the bad hand dealt to the Army by the SECDEF. In unfortunate circumstances, opportunistic commanders set ill-advised precedents by covering up readiness shortfalls; deception became a means of survival in bad commands.

We who survived the experience talked about the Army's problems while attending the Command & General Staff College and the Army War College. We shared our experiences and came to realize that they were not unique. Among the pearls of wisdom shared was learning what went wrong and appreciating the hard rules that govern in a bad command. Understanding those rules is important because they convey the differences between proper and improper conduct of duty, establishing the character of good and bad commands. In the final analysis these rules tell us something. They tell us when it is time to draw the line, to request a transfer, or to resign a commission – something that General Johnson failed to recognize when the time of decision was upon him.

Informal rules of survival, we learned, prevailed in units that had ceased to conform to Army Regulations for the management of property, training, and logistical support of units that had been cut loose from the umbilical cord of a functioning supply line. Dysfunctional behaviors became indicators of sick units. The following unethical practices, or rules of survival, characterized sick organizations:

- Bad management decisions at the top were covered up and their victims were held responsible for the sins of top management. Ethical commanders reporting accurately on the results of DOD's diversion of resources were relieved of command or given bad efficiency reports, leading to the elimination from the Army of soldiers of integrity.

- Non-combat ready equipment and equipment shortages were concealed. Lost, missing or broken equipment was covered up by falsification of readiness reports that concealed unit deficiencies.

- Higher-level commands and staffs institutionalized deception. Personnel managers covered up the diversion of qualified replacements to units in Vietnam while expecting subordinate battalion commanders to report their units as combat ready.

- Drastic reductions in fuel to support unit training resulted in curtailment of unit training, which reduced training readiness.

The practices described above – the behavior of those who resorted to deception to survive a bad command – violate Army Regulations. The admonition to dedicated, professional leaders is that when such patterns of behavior appear in the unit they must assess the alternatives to service in an organization operating beyond the pale. When honorable men and women encounter such practices, they have two choices: correct the problem, if it is localized, or depart units that indulge in the deceptive practices of bad commands. When all else fails, resignation from the service becomes the honorable approach to avoid the appearance of aiding and abetting unethical conduct.

I was put to the test when placed in command of a tank battalion in the 2nd Armored Division at Fort Hood, Texas, in 1975, where severe shortages continued to prevail for lack of funds to correct the problems created by years of inadequate support by the Department of Defense. Major General George S. Patton had just taken command of the division, when I assumed command of the 1st Battalion of the 67th Armored Regiment.

George Patton inherited a division that had suffered through all the problems and challenges we faced in Seventh Army. Equipment problems and personnel shortages were endemic in Army units of the period, part of the price paid because the Congress had not authorized sufficient funds to pay for the Vietnam War. The readiness and training of the Army steadily declined due to DOD's diversion of operations and maintenance funds. To maintain the illusion that the division remained combat ready, Patton's predecessor demanded that commanders falsify readiness reports to higher headquarters. The division looked good on paper and paid the bills by submitting false readiness reports – an outcome encouraged by Secretary McNamara's policies.

Following my assumption of command, I focused on training the unit and enjoyed the challenge of troop duty. Nevertheless, bad days and crises captured the trials and tribulations of Army service in the wake of our defeat in Vietnam. My staff soon explained the division's deceptive procedures – failing to report deserters and reporting inoperable equipment as combat ready. I told my staff that General Patton would never accept anything less than absolutely accurate reporting. I insisted they report the true status of the unit, regardless of practices that had prevailed in the past.

We reported accurately, and I noticed an immediate tension with the commander of the division's maintenance battalion. My people next complained that equipment returned by the maintenance battalion as supposedly fully operable had, in fact, never been repaired. I told my commanders and staff to collect the information for ninety days, and if we could document the trend, I would report the situation to the division commander. I intended to ensure that the problem was not an isolated incident.

We waited and documented the situation. At the end of ninety days my battalion staff summarized in a written report the flawed support given by our direct support maintenance battalion. It reflected a serious situation best characterized as institutionalized prevarication to conceal lack of readiness. The scam worked like this: The commander of the direct support maintenance unit would phone and ask what was needed in the way of equipment repairs to report the unit combat ready. The call would be made on the same day the readiness report came due. When the commander of the supported unit stated what he needed – for example, replacement of six tank engines, five transmissions, and six generators – the maintenance unit commander would tell him to report the unit as combat ready, and he would deliver the repaired equipment in the morning. "We'll stay up all night and repair the equipment" were his exact words.

Relying on the word of the maintenance battalion commander, my staff would submit a satisfactory readiness report only to discover later that the replacement equipment delivered the next day remained inoperable. Unfortunately, it would take time to discover the deception. Only after several days – the time required to install tank engines or change the transmissions – would we learn that the replacement equipment was inoperable, never truly repaired. The maintenance unit then stonewalled my protests: "It was working when it left here. You must have broken the engine during installation." We then had to start over from "square one" documenting a non-operational tank, opening a new job order, and waiting our turn to receive an operational replacement assembly.

I wrote out my resignation, stating that the division had institutionalized false reporting procedures and the maintenance battalion had concealed the problem by issuing broken replacement equipment as serviceable. I attached to my resignation the maintenance report prepared by the staff. I made multiple copies of both, providing information copies to each tank battalion commander, the brigade commander, the division support command commander, and the division commander.

I expected to find support for my actions from other commanders suffering from the same corrupted support system. To my amazement and disappointment, I found no support for my exposure of the division's unethical practices. Left to fight the problem by myself, the sidelines remained quiet as the fur flew. The sycophants who had bought into the false practices by falsifying readiness reports wanted no part of my stand opposing the corruption institutionalized in the division. They acted as if they didn't know me.

After delivering my resignation to the division's senior commanders, I went down to the motor pool. I assembled my officers and non-commissioned officers and read them my resignation. They cheered and applauded, a response typical of the rank and file in the Army. They wanted no part of organizations that relied upon unethical practices to accomplish the mission. They were elated that their commander supported them and sacrificed his career rather than tolerate unethical reporting of unit readiness.

My company commanders all insisted that they, too, would resign their commissions. I said that was not necessary. One resignation would suffice to cause a full investigation, conducted amid great venting of indignation by individuals party to the corrupt practices. When the smoke cleared, General Patton refused to accept my resignation, the assistant division commander for support retired, and we won a small victory. We received a new direct support maintenance company; thereafter, when we sent a tank engine for repair, it came back in working order.

I knew that General Patton would accept nothing less than full compliance with regulations. Curiously enough, soon after my offer of resignation, the former division commander, who had preceded Patton in command of "Hell on Wheels" and bore responsibility for the false readiness reporting procedures, was summarily relieved of the command of V Corps in Europe for false official reports. The chickens had come home to roost, and the Army had begun to repair wounds inflicted upon the integrity of the officer corps – second and third order outcomes of the bad management decisions and dishonesty of the former Secretary of Defense.

There are things far worse than resignation from the service. Far worse than the slings and arrows of unfounded criticism is setting a bad example in a position of responsibility, allowing one's actions to become a corrupt model for men and women in Army uniforms. The worst outcome for honorable leaders is not facing criticism from those who adopt corrupt practices; it is to dishonor the uniform and those they lead by dishonorable conduct – in this case by responding in an unethical manner to the decision of the SECDEF to cut the umbilical cord of support to field commands. Fortunately, my division commander trusted my judgment, investigated the charges, and found them to be true. In so doing he rewarded my decision to resign my commission. The Army had begun to turn the corner and honorable men again took the helm and began fixing problems of long standing in Seventh Army and the training base in CONUS.

Sink or Swim

by Brigadier General William J. Mullen III, USA (Ret.)

Army second lieutenants are rookies, tyros in a demanding profession. Though deemed proficient during the basic officer training required for assignment to a troop unit, the lieutenants have yet to be tested under realistic conditions. The Infantry School simply could not simulate the wide variety of conditions that a leader will encounter. The best that can be expected is to raise second lieutenants to the level of qualified apprentices with the potential to continue to learn through trial and sometimes error. Learning under actual conditions must take place in units. The Army tolerates mistakes made while trying something new during this on-the-job training in the unit. The Army refuses, however, to tolerate stupidity, carelessness that endangers lives and limbs, and ethical lapses.

It follows, then, that units become the places where second lieutenants learn how to lead. There they apply what the Army and life have taught them about people – leading, guiding, and coercing them as the situation dictates to accomplish a task under conditions that can be difficult and even dangerous. The lieutenants learn about the "Real World" while the Army learns about them – their character, their leadership abilities, and their physical endurance.

My first assignment to Germany came in 1960 in a place named *Wildflecken*. The unit was the 3d Battalion, 50th Infantry Regiment, a mechanized infantry unit equipped with M-59 armored personnel carriers. Captain John Weil, commander of D Company, assigned me to command his first platoon. I learned that the battalion would soon deploy to *Grafenwohr*, "Graf" to the soldiers, for weeks of training, culminating in an operational readiness test that would evaluate all aspects of battalion operations. In the Cold War environment, that important test aimed to ensure the battle readiness, at all times, of every unit during a tense period of the Cold War soon exacerbated by construction of the Berlin Wall.

I met my platoon at Graf when the men and the platoon's personnel carriers arrived by train. In those days a rifle platoon contained three rifle squads and a weapons squad. I was lucky. The First Platoon was blessed with highly experienced non-commissioned officers, or NCOs, in the positions of platoon sergeant and squad leaders. D Company went immediately into the field for tactical training. This totally immersed me in the tactical, logistical, and administrative requirements of leading a platoon. The time had come to sink or swim.

I did not sink. My training bore me in good stead. I learned. I stayed afloat. The key to my progress and avoidance of serious mistakes, however, was listening to those with more experience. My NCOs were great sources of information. Their advice was timely and reliable. This was particularly true regarding tactics. Not only were they good at tactics, but they had become experts on the terrain at Graf. They had been there and done that. They knew where armored vehicles, or tracks as we called them, could go and where they could not negotiate the terrain. They knew the good places to hide a unit. They knew the bottlenecks to movement and the shortcuts.

The battalion tactical exercises were important to my development. During a series of exercises, Captain Weil gave Delta Company and each of its platoons their missions. Each time, after receiving Captain Weil's order, I would return to my platoon area and huddle with the senior NCOs. Initially, it was my practice to describe the mission and the situation; I would then solicit ideas. Staff Sergeant Edelen, first squad leader, was particularly forthcoming with his views of what should be done. His ideas made sense. For the platoon's first few missions, I accepted his views and incorporated them into my platoon order.

A short time later, however, I broke that pattern. I again returned with the company commander's order and again I solicited advice from the senior NCOs. Sergeant Edelen again weighed in with his view. This time I did not accept his position, which made no sense to me. I disagreed with him and announced my decision for what the platoon would do and how we would do it. He didn't agree; he continued to press his view. I told him and the other NCOs that I had made my decision. I gave my order. The discussion ended.

What happened next has remained stuck in my mind to this day. Not one of the NCOs said a word. Their attitude, however, seemed to be one of satisfaction that their relationship with me had changed. They seemed relieved that I had overruled the advice. They seemed pleased that I was out of the nest and no longer dependent on them. I still had a lot to learn, but I would learn while swimming on my own. I was now the platoon leader – in fact, as well as in name. That was how the Army was supposed to work. They took their orders and moved out. The platoon accomplished its mission.

The most important event of my new profession up to that time occurred in that patch of woods at *Grafenwohr* where I took charge. The silent benediction I received from those four senior Infantry non-commissioned officers – Staff Sergeant Edelen, Staff Sergeant McKenzie, Sergeant First Class Mayo, and Master Sergeant Glenn – meant that I was a leader in fact as well as by title. Those men knew that I could swim without water wings. I knew it, too.

A Double Cold War Challenge
by Major James C. Corr, USA (Ret.)

In 1962-63 I served as Commander, C Company, 16th Signal Battalion (Army Area), a Seventh Army signal battalion stationed in Butzbach, Germany. The battalion was one of six such signal units providing vital area communications support throughout the Seventh Army's area of responsibility. The battalion consisted of four identical area signal companies, plus a headquarters company. Each area signal company consisted of a company headquarters, a signal center platoon with three lieutenants, and a cable construction platoon with one lieutenant. Overall the company had nearly 200 men, about 100 vehicles (mostly 2 ½-ton trucks), and around 65 large communications shelters mounted on 2 ½-ton trucks, all valued at about $500 million (most in the signal center platoon). In the preceding two years with the 16th Signal Battalion, I had led a signal center platoon in A Company and later commanded the Headquarters and Headquarters Company (HHC).

Just before I assumed command of C Company, the battalion had finished its Annual General Inspection/Command Maintenance Management Inspection (AGI/CMMI). In his exit interview, the Inspector General (IG) in charge of the inspection team stated: "C

Company was combat ready, but just barely." In the mission-essential, operational areas of telecommunications systems and facilities, the battalion S-3 (supported by the battalion commander) rated C Company's performance as the worst in the battalion. Facing those two challenges, I felt as though between a rock and a hard place.

To correct the "barely combat ready" rating, I used the first sergeant, platoon leaders, and platoon sergeants to get the company back on track. I told them they were the leaders most responsible for the low IG rating and for the S-3's poor assessment of our mission-essential operational areas. We promptly gave much needed emphasis to maintenance, personal attitude, morale, discipline, and appearance. The battalion required early morning motor stables, and I insisted that *all* leaders, not just lower ranking sergeants, attend. I also instituted a series of classes

Major James C. Corr, USA (ret.)

on all types of maintenance, to include vehicle and electronic, for my junior officers and senior noncommissioned officers. Technical personnel, such as the battalion motor and electronic maintenance officers and sergeants, conducted most of those classes, and the battalion

S-4 taught the sessions on supply and maintenance management. These classes taught the company officers and senior sergeants what to look for and how to correct problems. I then scheduled routine company inspections each Friday morning and afternoon (about an hour or so for each). The morning inspection focused on one major aspect of maintenance and the afternoon inspection concentrated on more general aspects of soldier skills: one afternoon on barracks inspection - with and without personal equipment layouts – another an inspection-in-ranks – sometimes with personal and crew-served weapons and then without. As those were the days of the 5 ½-day work week, I would reward the platoon or section getting my best rating with time off on Saturday morning – a "carrot and stick" approach.

For the more serious problem with the unit's telecommunications skills and performance, I resorted to a method I had learned a couple of years earlier. As a very junior platoon leader in the battalion, I quickly realized that I would never become a true technical expert as regards all the very complex types of equipments we operated and maintained, nor did I need to do so. I had learned the fundamentals, but not a lot of details, from the Signal Officer Basic Course. Back in 1960 and 1961 while our battalion was stationed at Fort Huachuca, Arizona, I teamed up with one of our senior warrant officers, CW4 George Ottinger, who had about thirty years Army service by then. George taught me (over much time) all the minimum essential technical details I would need to lead and manage all the technical enlisted men under my command and how to ensure these men actually knew the details they needed to perform in the field. Due to the length of time he had in the Army, he knew just about all aspects of the Army and he taught me much of that.

When our battalion deployed to Germany in mid-1960, I lost George but I did have a heads-up on how to do my job. When I later became the CO of the HHC, I met the most impressive senior warrant officer I would ever have the pleasure to know – CW4 Harvey E. Polk. Harvey was the battalion cryptographic officer, responsible for all the battalion crypto systems. He had well over 38 years Army service (his first fifteen years as a horse soldier) and really knew the Army inside and out. After his cavalry days, he became an Infantry noncommissioned officer in WWII and then a Signal noncommissioned officer during the Korean War and beyond. Later he received a warrant appointment and rose to the top grade. When I first got to know him, I learned that his favorite expression, in response to my asking "Harvey, can you get this done?" was "Sir, I'll guaran-Goddamn-tee you!" And he always did.

Knowing that our operational responsibilities and performance in telecommunications were most important, I needed to get my company moving on the right track – and quickly. I enlisted CW4 Polk to assist me in teaching my lieutenants and noncommissioned officers how to train and check on their subordinate enlisted men to ensure they performed successfully in their primary jobs. The company also needed additional tactical training regarding how to defend itself and its equipment. Again, CW4 Polk was very helpful, as were a couple of my most senior sergeants. I enlisted the help of the battalion S-3 (who had been my company CO in A company when I was a platoon leader) and members of his staff to explain to my junior leaders just why the battalion staff held C Company in such low esteem, and what we must do to improve its operational performance. These "outsider views" helped clarify problems that can be missed by individuals involved in day-to-day operations.

A further note: Knowing and being able to use Mr. Ottinger and Mr. Polk were gifts, and I was also fortunate later in my career to meet two more such experts. In 1966-67, I was assigned to the Headquarters, XVIII Airborne Corps Signal Section, as a plans officer. There I met CW4 Marv Swanson, who had well over thirty years service and taught me a wide range of subjects regarding being a Signal staff officer. Later on, in 1971-74, when assigned as the operations officer of the Allied Forces Southern Europe's Communications Signal Support Group, I met CW4 Bernie Hedges, who also taught me a great deal about NATO telecommunications equipment, systems, and procedures. I ran into Bernie again in 1977-79, when I was assigned to the headquarters of US Forces Korea. Assigned to the 1st Signal Brigade, he again proved very helpful in a number of ways.

The overall results of my effort (and much time) in C Company were the following:

- Improvements in maintenance and general soldier skills became apparent one year later during the next AGI/CMMI inspection. The IG leading the inspection team rated C Company as fully combat ready with fourteen of about thirty areas of inspection as worthy of note. The continuing performance of our varied equipment was consistently high and our inoperable equipment rates were the lowest in the battalion.

- As for mission-essential performance, we exceeded all the battalion commander's (and the S-3's) standards and expectations and were considered the best performing company in the battalion.

Some of the leadership lessons learned include the following:

- When faced with an under-performing unit, assess key weaknesses, identify sources of technical expertise, train subordinate leaders at all levels, hold them responsible for results, and reward performance.

- Signal officers do *not* have to be skilled technicians, nor should they try to be. But leaders must be able to check on their soldiers as they perform a wide range of tasks and not become the victim of a "snow job" from subordinates.

- Leaders must also learn how to train subordinates in primary job skills.

- Signal officers must quickly learn who they can trust to assist them in checking on unit performance, e.g., mission-essential tasks, maintenance, and soldier skills. Then they *must* trust them.

- When attending Army technical schools, Signal officers, especially junior ones, must pay close attention, take lots of notes, and ask lots of questions.

My use of the two very senior warrant officers to assist me was largely a matter of luck. Every Signal officer must nevertheless be able to identify senior personnel within the command who can teach the basics of telecommunications systems and facilities so the officer can perform competently as a leader.

FIVE

The POST COLD WAR STRUGGLE for PEACE

The end of the Cold War brought no end to the bitter struggle for peace. Terrorist groups formed during the long struggle to end French colonial rule in North Africa and Lebanon, combat the Soviet occupation of Afghanistan, and attack Israel on behalf of Palestinian Arabs launched a determined struggle against the United States, the West, and their allies. Despite the fact that the United States had led diplomatic efforts against French colonialism, supported Islamic insurgencies seeking to end the Soviet occupation of Afghanistan and Chechnya, fought ethnic cleansing aimed at Muslim communities in the Balkans, and worked tirelessly to bring about a peaceful settlement of Arab-Israeli differences, the radical Arab fundamentalists forming the core of terrorist groups that stretched from North Africa to South Asia and beyond saw the United States as their enemy. The newly acquired oil wealth of Arab States provided financial support for Arab fundamentalists in the guise of cultural and educational programs coupled with Islamic charities that acted as fronts to conceal funds for recruiting and fueling the terrorist war against the United States. Despite American diplomatic initiatives, military support, and foreign aid for Arab states in the region, Arab fundamentalists regarded America's democracy, modernity, and physical presence in the region as threats to their plans for toppling the region's "apostate" Arab governments and establishing a regional Islamist caliphate.

The following chapter records the leadership of members of the Class of 1959 who took part in hard-fought conflicts and the development of war fighting doctrine to secure America and its allies against terrorist groups by building in the region democratic states friendly to the United States.

— *The Editors*

ELDORADO CANYON:
The Story of the Libyan Raid

by Lieutenant General Thomas L. McInerney, USAF (Ret.)

Though not foreseen at the time, a 1984 directive from Joint Chiefs of Staff Chairman John Vessey to the regional commanders in chief (CINCs) contributed greatly to the success of Operation Eldorado Canyon. That directive called upon the CINCs to develop contingency plans for responding to rogue regimes or terrorist attacks against United States and allied forces. General Vessey's well-timed message reached his regional commanders at the height of the Cold War, with the strategic momentum beginning to move in favor of the U.S. and NATO due to the massive build up and modernization of America's armed forces during the Reagan administration. That modernization reversed the Carter administration's devastating impact on the U.S. military, which manifested itself in the loss of Iran to radical Islam, the seizure by radicals of our embassy in Tehran, and Desert One's failure to rescue the American hostages. No one in uniform, least of all General Vessey, wanted to see America humiliated like that again!

When the chairman sent his directive, I served as Deputy Chief of Staff for Operations and Intelligence at Headquarters, Pacific Air Forces, which made me responsible for devising the Air Force concept of operations and contingency plans for Pacific Command. The directive enabled the Pacific Air Forces to do Large Force Exercise training in the Korean Theater, where we simulated a 405 aircraft attack on Osan Air Base with the President of the Republic of Korea watching from a sofa at ground zero and joined by his entire leadership team. This exercise ordered the commanders of all Pacific wings to launch and recover from their home bases in the Philippines, Okinawa, Guam, and mainland Japan. It also required long-range air-to-air refueling, rapid weapons loading exercises, high rates of aircraft in commission, and constant real-time intelligence updates. The technology of the day and huge cultural limitations in the intelligence community made it difficult to release the special intelligence to the operational levels and complicated the latter task, but my dual responsibilities for operations and intelligence helped overcome the challenge.

Seeking to avoid failures such as Desert One, my team had the good fortune of superb support from the Commander in Chief of Pacific Air Forces (PACAF), General Jerry O'Malley, Lieutenant General Chuck Donnelly, Commander Fifth Air Force and Commander of U.S. Forces Japan, as well as Major General Fred Haeffner, Vice Commander PACAF. That failed operation haunted us, and we determined to never let it happen on our watch. That required realistic training under very severe conditions that were not risk free.

Though Red Flag, Tactical Air Command's realistic training exercises at Nellis Air Force Base (AFB), received all the publicity, I want to give you an example of the difference within PACAF, which launched 48 F15s – two squadrons – simultaneously in communications-out conditions while Red Flag launched only 12 F15s with full communications. We emphasized getting a strike force of 48 to 64 aircraft composed of F15s, F16s and F4s through a target complex in less than a minute so as to maximize saturation and minimize friendly losses. I mention these tactics and techniques because they were contentious in the Tactical Air

Forces (TAF), which consisted of the Tactical Air Command (TAC), U.S. Air Forces Europe (USAFE), and PACAF.

Even though we were conducting the most aggressive training, PACAF still received full support from its senior leaders. I mention all these facts because they became paramount in the success of ELDORADO CANYON later on, and that operation would not have succeeded but for the importation of the proven tactics and techniques developed and exercised in PACAF. Good fortune also intervened when Lieutenant General Chuck Donnelly became CINC, USAFE and brought me to Europe as commander of the Third Air Force in July 1985. Third AF comprised all the USAFE Wings in the United Kingdom. USAFE had two other numbered air forces – Sixteenth and Seventeenth – that covered southern and central Europe respectively.

Air space limitations would become a major challenge in densely packed Europe, but fortunately my two previous tours in the UK as Air Attaché (AIRA) and Vice Commander 20th Tactical Fighter Wing (F111s) at Royal Air Force (RAF) Base Upper Heyford had enabled me to know all the RAF leadership of the day. As the senior USAFE Commander in the United Kingdom (UK), my role had very high visibility, especially as I had responsibility for deploying the ground launch cruise missiles (GLCMs) into Central Europe as part of our Theater Nuclear Strike Force. In addition, my two F111 wings gave Third Air Force the largest theater nuclear forces in all of Europe combined. I mention this primarily to reemphasize the importance of personal relationships with our host and NATO allies.

While I was making my initial courtesy visit to UK Strike Command, Air Chief Marshall Sir David Craig, who later became the RAF Chief of Air Staff, asked me to provide target aircraft for his air defense fighters and radars. My predecessors had always refused this RAF request, but Sir David had been the Assistant Chief of Air Staff for Operations while I was the AIRA and I knew him well. Realizing this presented USAFE a historic opportunity, I immediately said yes without asking my CINC, knowing full well he would be delighted and that it fit with the direction I wanted to take Third Air Force in realistic training. The North Sea presented us with some superb training space for Large Force Employment and coupled with the UK's major exercise in the spring offered us a unique opportunity to accomplish my objectives and support the RAF. Little did I know that the RAF exercise was scheduled for the week after what would become the operation later known as ELDORADO CANYON. This good fortune allowed us to do the preliminary training with the RAF and the UK Joint Air Traffic Control leading up to ELDORADO CANYON, which required all the tactics and techniques we had developed in PACAF. General Donnelly was delighted when told of my Third Air Force exercise, but I needed the participation of the commanders of the other two numbered air forces as well, which required only that the CINC direct the Sixteenth and Seventh to take part.

Christmas 1985, three months after we started the run up to this exercise, the terrorists struck in Rome, followed by the bombing of a TWA aircraft over Athens and finally the April 1986 La Belle Discotheque bombing in Berlin. The UK's General Headquarters (GHQ), the equivalent to our National Security Agency (NSA), attributed the Berlin attack to Libyan ruler Colonel Muammar Qadhafi.

Between January and April 1986, the Joint Chiefs of Staff (JCS) tasked European Command to develop a series of response options against Libyan targets. The F111s of the 48th Tactical Wing at RAF Lakenheath received the primary wing assignment due to its precision strike and long-range all-weather capabilities. I therefore visited the wing weekly to fly or inspect various units and receive secret update briefings. My concerns were initially the non-value-added targets the

Joint Chiefs had selected and the lack of near real-time intelligence on the Libyan surface-to-air missile systems. To ensure the maximum operations security (OP SEC), I limited the planning cell to a very small number of wing personnel and remained for a time, the only Third AF officer cleared for the planning. Little did I know that the OP SEC in Washington would be the problem!

Meanwhile, I briefed all the wings in Third AF and worked with the RAF and UK Air Traffic Control on our Large Force Exercise (LFE) scheduled for 22 April 1986. This meant that each wing commander at the locations of the six flying wings had to prepare his forces for a maximum-effort launch of all his aircraft, which none had ever done. A wing normally flies only half its aircraft on a daily basis and schedules the remaining aircraft for maintenance. Simultaneously, the wings performed communications-out launches of aircraft working with the RAF Joint Air Traffic Control Agencies, a challenge ably met by our UK colleagues because RAF Strike Command wanted it done.

The U.S. forces could not have done this on their own initiative due to the task's complexity. Since I had already done this in PACAF, the learning curve was easier on my part. The wings of the Sixteenth and Seventeenth Air Force had to do the same thing on the Continent, but without making a maximum effort because they did not need all their planes airborne to meet the 405-aircraft goal for UK Strike Command. They did, however, have to fly from Spain and Germany to marshal over the North Sea, and each wing intelligence and operations division had to coordinate with the Third Air Force acting as the Joint Force Air Component Commander for air refueling and concept of operations planning. This was another valuable addition to the realistic training benefits gained from Large Force Exercises versus the isolated scheduling and planning a wing accomplished on a daily basis. This would also be the first time USAFE units had flown together in a coordinated attack plan since World War II!

Now, as the hour to execute drew near, the operation's major shortfall became having enough tanker aircraft to refuel the fighters coming from Spain and Germany to enable them to recover at their home bases. As a backup, we planned to recover them at UK bases and have transit alert quick-turn them for return to their home stations, not ideal but practical. As it turned out, we had more than enough tankers!

During all this planning for the joint exercise in the North Sea, the 5 April 1986 terrorist bomb exploded at the La Belle Discotheque in West Berlin, killing one American soldier and a Turkish national and injuring 200 people to include 63 U.S. soldiers of the Berlin Garrison. General Bernie Rogers, Supreme Allied Commander Europe (SACEUR) and Commander in Chief US Forces Europe (CINCEUR), was in Augusta, Georgia, watching the Masters Golf Tournament. Secretary of Defense Casper Weinberger directed Rogers to report directly to him in DC – immediately. Upon arrival he received an execute order in which the secretary personally ordered him to retaliate against Libyan targets with European Command (EUCOM) air and naval forces within his area of operations, which included the F111s from the 48th Tactical Fighter Wing (TFW) at RAF Lakenheath, EF111s from the 20th TFW at RAF Upper Heyford, plus the aircraft of two carrier battle groups (CVGs) – the carriers USS *America* and *Coral Sea* – located in the Mediterranean Sea.

On Friday, 11 April, I received notification to execute one of our contingency options and was told to meet with General Chuck Donnelly the next day. The 48th TFW Commander, Colonel Sam Westbrook, and I flew two F111Fs over to HQ USAFE at Ramstein AFB, Germany, to meet with the CINC and discuss our options. We met in the early afternoon, and General Donnelly told us that General Vernon Walters, USA (Ret.) was meeting with President Mitterrand of France at that moment requesting approval to fly over France with twelve attack

159

aircraft en route to Libya. Our other option required sending eight attack aircraft either over Spain or through the Strait of Gibraltar. In any case, we returned to Lakenheath that afternoon. At 2100 hours, I received a call from Sam Westbrook that we would execute the THIRD option, to which I responded that we only had TWO. As one quickly learns in these contingencies, change happens. Briefed early the next morning, I learned the new option would send 18 strike F111Fs and 4 EF111s from RAF Upper Heyford through the Straits of Gibraltar.

Tanker aircraft to form the air bridge to go this longer way returned as an immediate concern, though assured by USAFE that tankers would not be the problem. That proved the case, but the problem became where to bed all the arriving KC10 and KC135 tankers within Third Air Force. The National Command Authorities had downloaded the Nuclear Alert Force by sending many of the alert force tankers to the UK in support of Third Air Force's strike against Libya. According to the new plan, the Libyan strike would launch from four RAF bases in UK, rather than the planned two, and do so with a much larger force than planned. Fortunately, I had some great wing commanders and teams that responded magnificently with virtually no-notice planning.

Again our planning for the UK Air Defense Exercise proved critical to executing this strike because, for operational security reasons, we would give the UK Air Traffic Control Agency only thirty minutes notice, and it would be a communications-out launch unprecedented since WW II. In addition, the 48th Wing initiated a no-notice practice NATO Tactical Evaluation called Salty Nation so they could recall all their personnel without arousing suspicions in the local media, although some troubling leaks came out of Washington DC.

My next big task came Sunday evening when my Tanker Task Force (TTF) Commander advised me that he had women aircrews and U.S. law prohibited them from going into combat. He asked if he should start switching aircrews to download the women. I immediately said we would not change anything and go as formed aircrews. We had no time for foolish social changes. We were going to war as we had trained which brought a big sigh of relief.

The next challenge facing me as the Third Air Force Commander was moving all the aircraft into the Mediterranean without disclosing our plans to either Russian trawlers lurking off the UK or the Libyans themselves. When the TTF commander said the tankers would file an international flight plan, I asked if the Libyans would not receive the filing and possibly learn of our intentions. He said they would be excluded but I stated the other Arab nations would tell them off line, with a resulting loss of surprise. I again asked the TTF how we got the Mildenhall SR71 down there for their daily pictures, and he asked a major to come out from behind his classified office to tell me. This chap had obviously been working flat out for days because he looked very tired. He said the SR71 crew had flown on an international flight plan to Lands End in the western part of UK and cancelled their clearance and flew under visual flight rules. That posed no problem for them as they flew at 80,000 feet, but our strike force would be down around 30,000 feet, an altitude loaded with commercial airliners. Already late in the day, we had no choice. Also, we had radars on the fighters and tankers to assist our visual lookout. My final concern was the tanker-refueling plan for the increased number of fighters and tankers as well as launching from four different air bases. I found his briefing to be very complicated and asked him to brief the squadron commanders who were going to lead their flights against the three targets in Libya.

The three were the following: the Azziziyah Barracks, Colonel Gaddafi's headquarters where all the planning for terrorism occurred; Tripoli International Airport, from which flew its terrorists in Russian-made IL76s; and the swimming pool at Sidi Balal, where Libya trained terrorist frogmen. When briefed at Lakenheath, the squadron commanders asked the Tanker Task Force Commander to tie the tankers and fighters together for the whole mission at takeoff. In a remarkable degree of flexibility and tactical expertise, he agreed. That meant for the first time in a combat operation we would be transferring 1.5 million pounds of fuel airborne by using the new KC10s as mother aircraft that were themselves refueled by KC135s. This was a remarkable achievement in the annals of tactical airpower and it was really never highlighted for its success and tactical brilliance to the best of my knowledge.

My next challenge became notifying the UK Air Traffic Control authorities that we would be launching communications-out from four Third Air Force bases commencing at approximately 1830 on 14 April. I had been told that Prime Minister Margaret Thatcher had approved the launch, but I did not know whom she informed in the UK chain of command. I decided that the security of our launch was so important that I would have my Director of Operations personally notify the Air Traffic Control authorities of the launch 30 minutes prior to our first launch. I did not notify the RAF Chief of Air Staff or anyone else for fear of igniting a firestorm of questions. This was an important decision, and it upset some of the special relations I had with the RAF.

Finally, I prepared to welcome USAF Chief of Staff General Charlie Gabriel and his wife Dottie at 1630 hours on launch day. For this visit, laid on a year in advance, we kept to our schedule of events in order to minimize the chances of compromise and to continue our tactical deception. The Chief did brief the F111F aircrews at Lakenheath before they stepped to their aircraft and gave them a good pep talk. A former Army quarterback under the legendary Colonel Red Blaik, he gave an excellent talk, and we then watched the first launch of the eight aircraft that had the longest route to travel before they attacked Tripoli Airport from the south to ensure that on egress they would be heading towards the Mediterranean Sea. We also watched the Salty Nation exercise aircraft being launched, a marvelous bit of deception as BBC TV cameras were on the end of the field filming all takeoffs. We then went over to Mildenhall to observe the tankers, which shocked us as they took off in a direction opposite to the one planned. It turned out that the KC 10s, at maximum gross weight, changed plans when the wind shifted, a necessary decision but one greatly complicating the communications-out link for navigation purposes, which enabled this launch to be successful. Again, good fortune remained with us as the BBC crews at Mildenhall had gone to dinner thinking the action was at Lakenheath, which meant they missed the biggest tip off because the USAF had never launched 17 KC10s in one formation before. This launch would have definitely been on the BBC evening news, possibly compromising the tactical surprise essential to minimizing our losses. The Chief and I next went to my office and called the Chairman of the JCS, Admiral Crowe, to inform him of the launch of twenty-four F111Fs (eighteen primary and six spares); four EF111 electronic jammers (three primary and one spare); seventeen KC10 tankers; and thirteen KC135 tankers. The armada was on the way!

Admiral Crowe then asked if we knew that the Libyans had moved the IL76s and did we want to change the targets. The Chief looked at me and asked if we should change the targets and I said: "CHIEF WE ARE NOT CHANGING ANYTHING!" And that is what he told the Chairman. Thank God the Chief respected my judgment because changes would have created chaos. By the way I have no problem with the Chairman getting the daily all-source intelligence, but I swore I would work to ensure the combat aircrews got it simultaneously in the future. I must confess I never achieved that, but it did get better.

So as not to arouse suspicion, we continued our evening social schedule and after dinner went to the Lakenheath Command Post to listen to the attack sequence. The first radio contact we heard was when the lead squadron commander called "Feet Wet," meaning he had dropped his four 2,000-pound laser-guided bombs on Azziziyah Barracks at Colonel Gaddafi's quarters. We had no idea of his location because he and his East German bodyguards moved around every night. As it turned out, he was in the tent next to his quarters, which was to be attacked by the number two aircraft, which accidentally chose the wrong radar aim point and did not drop because of the danger of collateral damage. All aircraft attacked as planned except for the seventh plane sent against Azziziyah, which we think was hit by one of the 70-plus surface to air missiles the Libyans fired or his terrain following radar malfunctioned and he hit the water at 525 knots. In any case, we lost both of its two brave crewmembers.

Early in the morning, General Gabriel and I, accompanied by several of his senior staff, welcomed all the aircraft after this twelve-hour mission. It was an almost flawless mission executed in minimum time, and it certainly told the world we would not tolerate terrorist attacks. While debriefing the aircrews and viewing their video cameras, I received a call from the deputy to the CINC, who told me that the Chief could not take any of the video film back to Washington until Gen. Rogers had seen it. Needless to say, I told him to tell the Chief that and a long conversation ensued. In any case the Chief took the film back and became a hero in the eyes of Admiral Crowe because the overcast above Libya had obscured both the video satellites and SR71 film of the bomb damage. The F111's video cameras showed the exact bomb impact points. When the Chief walked into the "Tank," he found all the Service Chiefs distraught because they had nothing to show President Reagan until General Gabriel arrived with a complete debrief that soon went on worldwide TV after its viewing by President Reagan in the White House. The rest is history.

NOTE: I have not discussed all the work accomplished by the four U.S. wings and the RAF, a magnificent story requiring a separate book. To the best of my knowledge, none of what I have described here has ever been documented, but it could not have happened unless General Vessey started the ball rolling on long-range contingency planning two years prior.

A Commander's Perspective

by General Frederick M. Franks, Jr., USA (Ret.)

During the 1991 Gulf War, General Franks commanded the armor-heavy VII Corps that sent the equivalent of five American and British armored divisions smashing into fourteen Iraqi and elite Republic Guard formations in the highly successful "left hook" with which the U.S.-led coalition shattered Iraqi defenses in only a hundred hours and sent Saddam Hussein's forces in full flight out of Kuwait and back to safety in Iraq.

In a 1996 essay entitled "Battle Command: A Commander's Perspective," General Franks reflected on his command experience, which included an armored cavalry squadron and regiment, an armored division, and the VII Corps, before taking his command to Kuwait and achieving a victory some regard as "unmatched in modern warfare."

"In this slightly modified version of an article that first appeared in Military Review, *General Franks defines the three components—character, leadership, and competence—that he regards as essential to skillful battle command.*
—The Editors

"Don't worry, General, we trust you," a soldier in 3d Armored Division said to me a few days before we attacked into Iraq. That meant many things to me that day – and still does. That soldier trusted me to do my job as corps commander just as I trusted him to do his. Soldiers have every right to expect (trust) that their leaders know what they are doing. Trust, I believe, is the basic bond of leadership. One of the ways commanders build that bond is by demonstrating skills in battle command.

Battle command is defined in the 1993 US Army Field Manual (FM) 100-5, *Operations*, as *"the art* of motivating and directing soldiers and their leaders into action to accomplish missions. Includes visualizing the current and future state [both enemy and friendly]. . . then formulating concepts of operations to get from one to the other at least cost [to accomplish the mission]."[1]

* * * * *

Let me add a few personal observations about battle command. These are but highlights on such a rich subject area and are certainly not meant to re-write Army doctrine, which is very good but perhaps not so focused on battle command. I hope these thoughts will prompt ideas from other leaders with operational experience in battle command at all command echelons.

Battle command means *action*. It means accomplishing the mission at least cost to your troops in land operations – the tough unforgiving arena that is land combat. It requires of battle commanders a lifetime of practice and study to be ready for those minutes, hours, days or years of execution in actual operations. Actual battle is the great auditor of how well prepared the battle commander really is. That arena is no place for amateurs. In combat operations, battle command means seeing what is now, visualizing the future state or what needs to be done to accomplish

[1] US Amy Field Manual 100-6, *Operations* (Washington DC; US Government Printing Office, June 1993), 2-14.

the mission and then knowing how to get your organization from one state to the other at least cost against a given enemy on a given piece of terrain. To do this, you must be a skilled battle commander at any level-tactical, operational or strategic; in any type of command – single service, joint and/or combined; and in both war or MOOTW [military operations other than war].

I believe being a skillful battle commander has three components: character, leadership skills for your particular organization and competence.

Character in battle commanders counts. It is the key basis for trust. It gives leaders the moral force so necessary for soldiers to trust them in tough spots in battle. Courage, integrity, physical and mental strain, dependability, toughness, physical and moral fitness and loyalty to subordinates really make a difference. Being a battle commander of soldiers requires a lifetime of constant character development, sacrifice and self-discipline. In battle, it means being with soldiers, feeling their pride and their pain and sharing the hardships and the danger but then having the courage to go on and make the decisions to act at least cost to them. You have to feel it all, but you must be able to decide and commit the unit to action. You must feel the pain, but you must also have the courage to make decisions that may cost some of your soldiers' lives to accomplish the mission.

You have to know yourself. Character means having a sure confidence in yourself and who you are. Then you must have the courage to be who you really are, even in the face of modern battle, with its external pressures such as instant media coverage of operations, post-action second-guessing and instant judgment by others of the commander's place in history. It is not an easy thing, this retaining your own sense of self in a culture that demands obedience in battle. For example, in military hierarchies, leaders do a lot of agreeing with their commanders – and for good reason. On the battlefield, their commanders expect to get swift and effective compliance to orders. But what if you have a problem with the proposed solution? How do you maintain your sense of self if you have to continually compromise your honest judgments?

It is a good question and one every commander must answer. If you are lucky, you will serve with commanders of character who will be sensitive to that and will sound out subordinates before making a decision when the situation permits – a battlefield habit of Generals Robert E. Lee and George S. Patton Jr. that built an enormous loyalty. Then, having had your say, you follow the decision and execute. Yet, you will not always be so fortunate. That is when character shows up in commanders. If it does not, you compromise yourself and your soldiers. Each battle commander has to answer this basic dilemma. *Soldiers know how you answer.*

Battle commanders must also be strong when the going gets tough and in the face of casualties. At those times, they must rise to new levels and lead their units to do the same. Senior tactical battle commanders must have the toughness and courage to decide, and then commit their units to a course of action long before the battlefield outcome is assured. Good historical battles that come to mind include Brigadier General John Buford's and Major General George Meade's decision to fight at Gettysburg; General Dwight D. Eisenhower at Normandy in June 1944; and General Douglas MacArthur and X Corps at Inchon, Korea in 1950.

Then battle commanders must have the skill to assure a successful outcome by actively leading their organizations to victory at least cost. Battle commanders with soldiers in direct contact with the enemy, like their soldiers, must reach inside themselves for that inner toughness to go on in the face of casualties and with the outcome of the fight in real doubt. Retired Lieutenant General Harold G. Moore's and Joseph L. Galloway's *We Were Soldiers Once and Young* comes to mind. To go on, you must have that battle commander fiber of toughness, some inner steel and self-control. Yet, it is okay and sometimes necessary to show deep feelings and to get angry, as long as you are true to yourself and your soldiers and are in control of yourself in battle. You must be bold without the arrogance that shuts off listening, even in the heat of battle, and makes you set yourself up as infallible – a real vulnerability later in a campaign following a string of successes – or later blame subordinates for your own shortcomings.

As success and failure in battle or MOOTW become immediately public, pressures on character in battle commanders will also grow as will conflicting views on their reputations. Real battle commanders care most about their reputations with their soldiers. They know that is what really counts. One major factor influencing reputation is whether battle commanders focus most of their attention internally or externally. How, for example, do commanders look out for their troops with the next-higher headquarters? What do they do when things go wrong or not exactly as planned? Do they blame subordinates for their own shortcomings, or do they do as General Bruce C. Clarke used to say, "When things go wrong in your command, start wading for the reason in increasingly larger concentric circles around your own desk"?[2]

To be a successful battle commander, you must work at it and sacrifice yourself for others. That means denying self for the mission and soldiers. There is no room for a "me first" attitude in battle commanders leading American soldiers in battle. *The spotlight should be on the led not the leader.*

Battle command *is* being secure, standing for something worthwhile,

---

[2] *Leadership: Quotations from the Military Tradition,* edited by Robert A. Felton (Boulder, CO: Westview Press Ind., 1990), 238.

taking a stand to do what is right for the mission and troops, even though it might cost us professionally. *It is not* being threatened by new ideas or questioning by subordinates in the heat of battle. It means to lead troops is to also serve them. It means having the personal touch of remembering individual soldiers and always having time for them especially when you have asked them to do a tough mission. For battle commanders, it means really caring for soldiers but also having the courage to act when necessary to put them in harm's way to accomplish the mission.

If that sounds demanding, it is. Duty as a battle commander is the toughest taskmaster and demands character. We do not seem to talk much anymore about the character element of battle command, which I think is a mistake. It matters and it is combat power.

Along with strong character, battle commanders need *leadership* skills. These skills have both intellectual and human dimension components. First, this means knowing how to make the various parts of the organization work together to complement one another in battle. In other words, how to focus the arms and services in various organizations in the right combination to generate combat power to get the mission done and done right at least cost. In short, leadership means getting the units to the right place at the right time in the right combination on increasingly dispersed battlefields where you will only want to physically mass forces at the last moment. That is different for a platoon than for a corps, an army or a joint TF. It means understanding organizational dynamics and people.

Battle command of smaller tactical echelons of platoons, companies and battalions is more direct with rapid assessment and decision and then quick response from orders to execution. Leadership of large tactical formations such as brigades, divisions, corps, armies or JTFs requires considerable organizational skills and more and more knowledge of

170

technology and history. Things happen more slowly, yet more and more information is available. It means knowing, for example, the effects of orders – how long it takes for a particular type unit to execute after an order is given. It means the more senior battle commander must have an understanding of what subordinates are doing and how long that takes, especially when the subordinates are acting on their own initiative. It means having knowledge of an expanded battle space that has both physical assigned theater dimensions and an intellectual dimension that often transcends the theater, is even civil-military, and that impacts decisions. It means having the self-discipline to know when to decide and when not to decide, even in the face of an increasingly clearer picture of the battle. This is why the US Army insists that commanders go through rites of passage, demonstrating skills at one echelon before moving onto the next.

Leadership in battle is also about decision making. That is why we give commanders wide latitude in the execution of their responsibilities. We trust them. Take a look at the wording in promotion orders. We also demand they set the right command climate – getting the whole organization involved in being a winner on the battlefield so everyone wants to contribute. Pride in one's unit and loyalty to the unit count in battle. Much of that has to do with when, how and where you decide.

Battle command leadership means skill in when you decide. In smaller tactical echelons, decision making is a one- or two-person operation, and the tempo of decision making is fairly high – the number of decisions made overtime, especially in battle, is high. The need to decide at these echelons of command is normally quite obvious and does not cause much deliberation. However, the more senior you become the fewer decisions you need to make and the more people and staffs you have available to help you. Moreover, advancing technology will give an increasingly clearer electronic picture of reality. The need to decide is not so obvious. In addition, especially in land warfare, the consequences of your decisions affect much more complex organizational relationships and thus, once made, they are hard to retrieve even if you get a better idea later.

Most often, as a senior tactical commander during battle, I found I was "deciding to decide." In other words, I had to ask myself, did I need to intervene, did I need to make a decision at that point or did I need to add reinforcements to help a subordinate unit accomplish the mission I gave them or give them time and reinforcements to exploit an initiative they created, such as getting fuel to Major General Ronald Griffith's 1st Armored Division the morning of 27 February 1991 to continue the attack I ordered and their own initiatives against the Republican Guard Forces Command (RGFC) Medina Division? Most often, the answer was I did not need to intervene, even though I knew I always must have options available. Battle commanders and their staffs must constantly generate options; what they are trying to do is run the enemy out of options, an insight I gained in BCTP [Battle Command Tactical Planning] and which we included in FM 100-5.

As a senior tactical commander, you really only get to make a few key decisions, so you might as well try to anticipate when those will come, and then focus on them and do not dissipate your energies on decisions best left to subordinates. You also get to pick your battles or seize the initiative from the enemy. Senior battle commanders must learn that much of their energy is spent in anticipating or forecasting the next battle and the one after that. They must be involved in the present but remain detached enough to be able to forecast the future. Often, their biggest choice is when to decide and when not to. Being capable of rapid synthesis of information and then having the organizational feel for that command echelon and what is and is not possible overtime, terrain and a given enemy, also helps you know when you need to decide.

Deciding when to decide is also where character helps. Be sure in who you are and trust that your subordinates and troops will do what they need to do.

Besides *when* you decide, *how* you decide is also important. How you decide means, among other things, balancing in battle the right mix of your own command guidance with giving subordinates room to use their own initiative or at least identifying where you want tight control and where you do not. For example, during *Desert Storm*, in my statement of intent, I made a point of the difference between the breach, where we needed tight control, and the envelopment, where there was a need for much less control and more room for initiative.

How you decide also means involving your subordinate commanders. How much consultation do you want? Do you want to sound out subordinates? Can you do war-gaming? Do you have time for that? Remember Lee at Chancellorsville to Lieutenant General Thomas "Stonewall" Jackson: "What do you propose to do?" Jackson, "Go around here." Lee, "With what?" Jackson, "With my whole corps." Talking to subordinates, if you are in the habit of doing so and have built a tight family team, is done in short word bursts and does not take long. You want to build consensus and thorough understanding of your intent not by the path of least resistance, but by explaining and arguing the best solution approach yourself in an effort essentially to teach it to subordinates. Someone asked me how much of my time was spent teaching as VII Corps commander during *Desert Storm*. I said over 50 percent. I spent a considerable amount of time up to crossing the line of departure visiting subordinate commanders and teaching my intent and looking their battalion and brigade commanders in the eye to see if they understood and if they and their soldiers were ready. What I was doing was ensuring that commanders understood and had confidence in the plan-building consensus – not by compromise but by teaching the plan myself – and embedding understanding, if you will, and listening to them so I could make adjustments as necessary.

During battle, I continued to visit commanders to both listen and direct always from a common understanding because we were face-to-face. I was not unusual. We all did that. No one stayed in his CP. This practice was true in *Just Cause* as well. Because land combat will continue to be tough, brutal, full of friction and with unpredictable enemies, commanders will want to be on the battlefield with their troops and not in their CPS. They need to be *upfront*. As our Army experiments with more precise, electronically displayed situational awareness made possible by technology, we must watch what types of input influence our mind's eye picture of reality and where that picture requires the commander to be. For instance, in making decisions during *Desert Storm*, I got maybe 20 percent of my information during battle from CP input, 50 percent from being up front on the battlefield and getting assessments from my commanders and 30 percent from embedded memory of education and training.

Commanders of smaller tactical echelons do not have the time or usually the freedom to move around the battlefield for a whole lot of consultation. Nor is that necessary or expected by subordinates. More senior commanders, though, have the time to do that if they can forecast and anticipate, because they usually are thinking in blocks of hours and days, rather than in minutes or single hours, as is characteristic of lower-tactical echelons. Additionally, senior commanders have a lot of nondecision making time on their hands during battle.

Thus, I predict commanders will continue to be out and around the battlefield. Information age technology producers need to understand ground commander behavior and make the technology help. They should not build systems designed to keep battle commanders information prisoners of what we now call CPs. Moreover, the Army must ensure we do not invent future battle command requirements to fit a worn-out C2 engine. That is what our battle lab and Force XXI experiments are all about!

Therefore, how you decide means involving subordinates in decisions, whenever possible, because their judgments and assessments are the most valuable you will get. For some, especially those commanders at battalion level and below, it means seeing, listening, quickly imagining what you cannot immediately see, and then deciding – sometimes in nanoseconds, sometimes without much consultation. For senior tactical commanders, it means doing a lot of listening, gathering information and seeing what is going on in the present but having the discipline to remain detached enough to imagine or forecast the future or what you cannot see. Senior commanders deal more with what they can imagine and what they cannot see. They must see the present, imagine the future – both friendly and enemy – as it should be to accomplish the mission and then figure out the best way to get from one state to the other at least cost to their soldiers. They must see in their "mind's eye" what others cannot. That is where the long years of practice and study, as well as information about the reality of the present, cause your intuitive senses to be able to see what others cannot.

It also means adopting a scheme of maneuver that allows you the widest range of options and then keeping your forces balanced so any of those options are available to you. Then you wait until the last possible moment to decide – but not so long that your unit cannot execute – because you want to always be at least one move ahead of the enemy. Of course, this sometimes frustrates staffs because they want early decisions so they can get their considerable coordination work done at a reasonable pace – sometimes staffs even think their commander is indecisive. What you are really doing is outthinking the enemy and then outfighting him. Bulldog determination of units in battle comes primarily from commanders who, when they do decide, make the decision, stick by their actions and do not constantly change their minds. I always tried to establish what I called a "GICOD," or good idea cutoff date, and also tried to ensure orders to subordinate commanders lasted at least 12 hours during *Desert Storm*. Force of command in battle is determined mostly by how you decide, how you communicate that decision and whether you make it stick. That is why tactical commanders must be out and around the battlefield, even in the future which will have more apparent electronic reality. This also applies to operational and theater strategic commanders. If they are going to make tactical-level decisions or operational and strategic decisions with tactical consequences, they had better get out of their CPs, go have a look around, and talk to the tactical commanders involved.

Thus, all commanders must have the skills to get the information they need. They must drive PIR (priority intelligence requirements). Gaining information they need during battle is different from deliberate planning. That is why we say "fighting is not planning." That is why General William T. Sherman said, "It is not who knows the most but who does the best." Then commanders must decide to decide, decide, make it stick, don't look back, and communicate that decision to the right places in the right way to get it executed. Then they must follow through because nothing happens solely because they ordered it.

Finally, *where* you do all that, along with how and when you decide and how you disseminate the solution, is also important. In battle, commanders normally make decisions where they are, as opposed to waiting until they get to some freed place such as a CP. This is especially so when other commanders are present because the face-to-face dimension reduces probabilities of misunderstanding and gives subordinates more time. In battle, commanders should never order their subordinates away from their units for a meeting; they should go to their subordinates. Simultaneously keeping everyone informed, not overlooking anything major because your staff was not physically present to help you, and ensuring continued balance of your moving formation, such as coherent relationship of the various parts of your organization to each other as they all are moving is difficult but is an essential battle commander leadership skill.

Leadership skills also have a human dimension that is inseparable from the character element already discussed. This dimension shapes and influences how you build teams, which is often done very quickly today as forces are put together for missions difficult to forecast far in advance. Building teams in large organizations means knowing, essentially, how to build a family where everyone's role is vital to success. This means leading subordinate commanders. They are strong and proud soldiers – otherwise they would not be good commanders – and they all want the best for their units. I think you do this in battle by assigning missions according to commander and unit skills. That lets units all contribute in their own way to the victory. Building teams also means treating everyone with dignity and respect during an operation that mixes units, both Active and Reserve, and puts soldiers in unfamiliar cultural environments. It also means getting units to bounce back quickly after a tough battlefield loss. Thus, building and rebuilding teams is continuous and means battle commanders move around the unit constantly before and during battle.

Only about 40 percent of USAREUR VII Corps was the *Desert Storm* VII Corps. We had a new team to build at corps level, as we drew units from USAREUR and the United States, both Active and Reserve Components. All my subordinate commanders had the same challenge, because their *Desert Storm* units were different from their peacetime or garrison organizations. For example, General Grffith added a brigade from the 3d Infantry Division (Mechanized), plus changed leaders in a brigade. Brigadier General Robert McFarlin expanded VII Corps' Corps Support Command from 7,500 soldiers in Germany to more than 25,000, with most additions from RC units in FORSCOM. Brigadier General Creighton Abrams added thee new brigades to one original VII Corps Artillery brigade to form corps artillery. Colonel Samuel Raines added six battalions and two group headquarters to the 7th Engineer Brigade. Colonel Richard Pomager added National Guard battalions to the 14th Military Police Brigade. Colonel Richard Walsh added much needed signal units to expand the desert capability of the 93d Signal Brigade.

Thus, you must build teams and make rapid assessments of your new command team. Early and frequent visits to new team members help because you can see them in action during the sometimes tense leadership situations of deployment and get an idea as to how they would command in battle. For example, my early visits to former V Corps units with 3d Armored Division Commander General Funk and 42d Artillery Brigade Commander Colonel Morris J. Boyd gave me insights I would later recall in deciding their missions because I had confidence they would succeed. In the case of Funk, because he was an immediate subordinate and I would talk directly to him, my visit helped in our mutual ability to communicate commander-to-commander in battle in short word bursts. As units join you, such as happened to VII Corps in Saudi Arabia with the 1st Cavalry Division and 1st United Kingdom Armoured Division, you must go see them and make them part of your unit, assess their capabilities quickly, and then employ them accordingly.

How do you get the unit to respond? What techniques do you use to peak the unit to a particularly challenging mission, especially when soldiers and units are tired or have just suffered a setback or, worse, a tactical defeat? How do you get a unit ready for combat with few combat veterans in it? You must know how to motivate and rally the unit to do what needs to be done. You must be sensitive to how long your units are on the attack and husband the strength of soldiers and leaders for the decisive moments in the campaign so it is not dissipated on other less important activities. Senior battle commanders pick their battles over time and arrange them to gain maximum advantage for their own troops and to accomplish the mission. You also must be aware that tired units behave differently in battle and may cause you to intervene with help that you would not have to give had they been fresh. The language you use and the way you communicate are important in battle. You try to tailor your communication techniques to fit the effect you want to have.

Battle commanders at all echelons also form their units' identities – their characters in battle. Remember the old saying: A unit is the reflection of the commander! A unit has a spirit and an identity that you form by being out and around during battle – make the unit one with yourself like a family. Build winners! Soldiers want to be on a winning team and will fight to keep it that way. That will also inform your intuitive judgments and give you a sense of the art of the possible and the cost of a course of action. A unit's character also includes discipline and subordinating self for the good of the unit, especially when the going gets real tough—"doing what is right when no one is looking." I was proud of VII Corps soldiers and leaders who had the self-discipline to check weapons, clean air filters, do the fundamentals well, who were aggressive, tough and relentless in pressing the attack and then did what was right in treatment of enemy prisoners of war and refugees immediately after battle.

Finally, *competence* is also an integral part of skill in battle command. It means knowing our profession, the craft of it all, and the nuts-and-bolts details. It is inseparable from leadership. Knowledge of the craft of our profession lets battle commanders execute their command responsibilities better because they can use all available tools. In sum, competence is quite simply knowing your job as well as your soldiers know theirs.

It all means knowing the technical capabilities of your unit – weapons, logistics, electronic warfare, aviation and movement on terrain. Tactics often is determined by the capabilities and limitations of weapon systems and how quickly units can move from one place to another. You have to work hard at this. As VII Corps' commanders during *Desert Storm*, we needed to know about the MIA1 Abrams tank, Bradley Fighting Vehicle, multiple launch rocket system, Army Tactical Missile System, Patriot missile, Apache helicopter, mine plows and rollers, Global Positioning System (GPS), Joint Surveillance and Target Attack Radar System, HAWKEYE and Pioneer, just to name a few. Go fire the weapon systems, qualify on a tank and learn new systems as they are fielded from hands-on experience.

All of us needed to know desert terrain. Besides the leaders' "recon" and the lessons learned we got from XVIII Airborne Corps, my aide, driver and I spent considerable time in our HMMWV [high-mobility multipurpose wheeled vehicle] in the desert so I could personally recalibrate my European time-distance judgments of unit moves to the desert and get a feel for navigation with GPS. I was not unusual. Moving around the corps also let me visit and listen to leaders and soldiers, observe training and get a firsthand impression of their mental and physical capabilities and limitations in that environment as they prepared for the operation.

Besides knowing systems capabilities, commanders must know how all the parts fit together on the battlefield to produce combat power. They must have the competence to focus that combat power time and again, to know what parts are quickly reusable and what parts take longer to move and concentrate, to understand staying power and to designate points of main effort and where they want economy of force. On increasingly dispersed battlefields with more and more precision-targeting capabilities, commanders will need to have the competence to rapidly and physically mass from dispersed formations at the last moment but in the right combination of units. They must know the difference between risk and gamble. I always use German Field Marshal Erwin Rommel's definitions in Desmond Young's excellent book, *Rommel: The Desert Fox*. Rommel says that risk — which he terms "operational and tactical boldness" — is a chance you take that if it does not work you can recover, while a gamble is a chance you take that if it does not work, the unit cannot recover.[3]

From my own experience, one other element of risk and gamble is that your next-higher commander should be in on the decision. If the risk does not work, you will normally be able to recover yourself; if the gamble does not work, your next-higher commander normally will have to commit resources to allow you to recover. You must have the courage to take a risk or to gamble when the situation demands. You must also know joint and special operating forces and how to employ both to

complement your own capabilities to accomplish the mission. Sometimes the rules for employment vary from theater to theater, as we

Lieutenant General Frederick M. Franks, Jr. VII Corps, briefs his subordinates, 1991.

[3] Desmond Young, Rommel: *The Desert Fox* (New York: William Morrow & Co., Inc., 1987), 230.

found out with the rules for air-to-ground changing considerably from NATO to US Army Central Command in 1990.

Competence also demands considerable thinking and communication skills in battle. Battle commanders must be direct in their verbal transmissions and use soldier language with the doctrine. They should be especially precise when soldiers get tired or are under a lot of battle pressure. Sometimes they need to get dramatic in gesture or language to communicate intent. I used to smash my closed fist into my hand to show how I wanted to hit the RGFC with a massed three-division force, as opposed to poking at them one finger at a time.

During staff sessions, it does not hurt to "think out loud," another technique I learned from General Cavazos, because this helps the staff understand how you are approaching a problem and what information you find helpful. Competence also demands imagination. You must be able to see in your mind's eye what others cannot and you must do this faster than your enemy. You must rapidly synthesize pieces and fragments of information into a coherent picture – commander's estimate; then possess a feel for when to decide and a willingness to act on that mind's eye picture when it is time. This takes considerable practice, and battle commanders should take every opportunity to work on this skill. This is also where boldness enters and real battle commanders stand out. This skill in synthesis and willingness to act takes a different kind of courage. It is the one competence that really separates battle commanders.

You also must know your enemy. Try to get into the enemy commander's head. In my own case, I visited our EPW camp to see Iraqi soldiers for myself. In addition, I tried to envision what the Iraqi VII Corps commander – with units to our direct front and between us and the RGFC – was trying to do. We thought his mission was economy of force and to tell the RGFC our direction of attack. We thought the

RGFC commander farther back was trying to defend from where he was to block our attack up the Wadi al Batin or defend a little farther west with a massed-position armor defense. That insight let us devise an attack plan that would accomplish our own mission and defeat the enemy's plan. You also learn about the enemy from other actions on the same battlefield. We got valuable insights from the Marines as a result of the Iraqi attack at Khafji. Most valuable of all were the lessons from Brigadier General John Tilelli and the 1st Cavalry Division from their combat actions in the Rugi Pocket, conducted to deceive Iraqi forces into thinking we were attacking up the Wadi al Batin. I always found it useful to keep a "red team" around who would think like our enemy. Such a practice keeps you sharp and competitive. Thus, you need to know the enemy, but you must neither overestimate nor underestimate him.

You also must know that combat power is, as our doctrine rightfully says, situational, relative and reversible.

You have to know your team. Some units do some things well; others do other things well. Who do you pick for what mission? Who does the breach? Can two USAREUR divisions operate side-by-side on a 40km front better than two divisions that are not habitual partners? What unit had the longest training time in the desert and was best practiced at long and rapid moves? What combination of units will accomplish the mission at least cost? In VII Corps, I settled on the final major unit task organization about mid-January 1991 and refused to change it because I wanted the team to get used to working together. How do you best integrate forces of another nation into your scheme of maneuver to give them a reasonable chance of success, and what US support do you give them?

We operate on land. Terrain appreciation is a vital component of battle command competence. You must see in your mind's eye your own forces and the enemy's on a given piece of terrain. That means knowing how to use that terrain to your own best advantage by studying maps, moving around the terrain yourself, having some knowledge of history (from a study of desert wars over time, I was convinced maneuver, control of the air and logistics were keys to victory) and having an appreciation of how precision-location technology and virtual reality can help you. The "art and science" parts of how we see the terrain will change for us in the future, but we will still need battle commanders to visualize their forces and those of the enemy on that terrain as they decide how best to win. Fighting a large land formation in the deserts of Iraq and Kuwait was much like naval surface warfare. We could take our "fleet" anywhere and did so while the Iraqis took theirs out and anchored it with short anchor chains. That, of course, is not true in all deserts nor for all enemies, just as it was not true in Central Europe in the old days, nor is it true in Bosnia today. But because tactical solutions frequently have much to do with terrain appreciation, it is an indispensable element in the battle commander's competence kit bag.

These then are a few thoughts on how character, leadership skills and basic competence go together to make successful battle commanders. They are not all-inclusive, given the space for this article. There are recent publications, briefings and seminars about battle command drawn from excellent work done by Major General Lawson Magruder, Brigadier General James P. O'Neal, Colonel Russell Honore and other NTC and JRTC O/Cs, by perceptions of senior O/Cs and by Colonel Michael Kain and the BCTP team members who watch and think about battle command every day. They are excellent and deserve reading and study.

Battle command is combat power. It is difficult to measure and quantify, but it is combat power nonetheless. These thoughts formed for me the basis on which I could judge whether I was up to my end of the agreement when that 3d Armored Division soldier said, "Don't worry, General, we trust you." *MR*

AUTHORS' BIOGRAPHIES

ABRAHAMSON, James L., Armor. Principal Assignments: 15th Armored Cavalry (Germany); Royal Armoured Centre (United Kingdom); Graduate School of International Studies (Switzerland); Department of Social Sciences (West Point); 11th Armored Cavalry (Vietnam); Combat Developments Command (Fort Knox); Command and General Staff College (Fort Leavenworth); Stanford University (California); Department of History (West Point); Army War College (Pennsylvania). Retired, Colonel, 1986.

COHEN, William A., USAF. Principal Assignments: 26th Bomber Squadron (Altus AFB); 11th Strategic Aeronautics Wing (Altus AFB); University of Chicago (Illinois); 609th Air Commando Squadron (Thailand); Aeronautical Systems Division (Wright-Patterson AFB); Resigned, Major, to join Israeli Air Force (Israel); Reactivated in United States Air Force Reserve; 445th Military Airlift Wing (California); Space Division (California), Industrial College of the Armed Forces (DC), Kirtland AFB (New Mexico); Public Diplomacy Special Action Group DOD (Pentagon); Headquarters, Air Force Systems Command (Andrews AFB); Headquarters, Air Force Material Command (Wright-Paterson AFB); Space and Missile Center (Los Angeles); Headquarters, Air Education and Training Command (Randolph AFB). Retired, Major General, USAFR, 1997.

COLBY, Nathaniel F., Signal Corps-Armor. Principal Assignments: 142nd Signal Battalion (Germany); 3rd Battalion, 40th Armor (Korea); 101st Airborne Division (Fort Campbell); 3rd Battalion, 37th Armor (Germany); 2nd Squadron, 17th Cavalry (Vietnam); Combat Development Command (Virginia); MSNE (University of Missiour); Armed Forces Staff College (Virginia); Defense Nuclear Agency (DC); 1st Battalion, 64th Armor (Germany); 21st Support Command (Germany); Headquarters, VIIth Corps (Germany); 2nd Readiness Region. Retired, Lieutenant Colonel, 1981.

CORR, James C., Signal Corps. Principal Assignments: 16th Signal Battalion (Fort Huachuca & Germany); Headquarters, Seventh Army (Germany); Headquarters, United States Army Security Agency (Arlington); 121st Signal Battalion (Fort Riley & Vietnam); 9th Signal Battalion (Fort Riley); Headquarters, XVIII Airborne Corps (Fort Bragg); Headquarters, 29th Signal Group (Thailand); Military Assistance Command (Vietnam); J6, NATO, Allied Forces Southern Europe (Italy); Modern Army Selected Systems Test, Evaluation & Review Activity — later changed to TRADOC Combined Arms Test Activity (Fort Hood); United Nations Command & U. S. Forces, J6 (Korea); Headquarters, XVIII Airborne Corps (Fort Bragg). Retired, Major, 1980. As Department of Army Civilian (DAC), 1981-1998: Headquarters, United States Army Forces Command (Fort McPherson); Force Design Directorate, United States Army Combined Arms Center (Fort Leavenworth); Headquarters, United States Army Europe (Germany); Force Development Support Agency, Department of the Army (Pentagon). Retired, GS-13, 1998.

FABER, Michael J., USAF. Honorary Member of the Class of 1959. Principal Assignments: 551st Headquarters Squadron (Otis AFB);

7272nd Air Police Squadron (Wheelus AFB Libya); Special Projects, Headquarters Squadron (Nellis AFB). Honorably discharged, Sergeant, 1969. Editors: The Class of 1959 gratefully acknowledged Mike Faber for his efforts to memorialize class member Humbert "Rocky" Versace and win for him a much-deserved Medal of Honor.

FRANKS, Frederick M., Jr., Armor. Principal Assignments: 11th Armored Cavalry (Germany); Columbia University (New York); Department of English (West Point); 2nd Squadron, 11th Armored Cavalry (Vietnam); Armed Forces Staff College (Virginia); OACS Force Development (Pentagon); Columbia University (New York); 1st Squadron, 3d Armored Cavalry (Fort Bliss); National War College (DC); Training and Doctrine Command (Fort Monroe); 11th Armored Cavalry (Germany); Seventh Army Training Command (Germany); Headquarters, United States Army Europe (Germany); Command and General Staff College (Fort Leavenworth); Office of the Joint Chiefs of Staff (Pentagon); 1st Armored Division (Germany); VII Corps (Germany and Kuwait); Training and Doctrine Command (Fort Monroe). Retired, General, 1994.

GRINALDS, John S., USMC. Principal Assignments: Rhodes Scholar (United Kingdom); 8th Marine Regiment (Camp Lejeune); Military Assistance Command (Vietnam); Fleet Marine Force (Pacific); DOD Systems Analysis (Pentagon); 1st Marine Regiment (Vietnam); White House Fellow (DC); Harvard University (Massachusetts); Manpower Department (Headquarters, Marine Corps); National War College (DC); 3rd Battalion, 8th Marine Regiment (Camp Lejeune), 2nd Marine Division (Camp Lejeune); 9th Marine Regiment (Okinawa); Supreme Headquarters, Allied Powers Europe (Belgium); Plans, Policy and Operations (Headquarters, Marine Corps); Office of the Joint Chiefs of Staff (Pentagon); Marine Corps Recruit Depot (San Diego). Retired, Major General, 1991.

HAIGHT, Barrett S., Signal Corps-Judge Advocate General Corps. Principal Assignments: 25th Infantry Division (Hawaii); 72nd Signal Battalion (Fort Huachuca); Dickinson School of Law (Pennsylvania); 1st Infantry Division (Vietnam); Department of Law (West Point); 8th Infantry Division (Germany); Command and General Staff College (Fort Leavenworth); University of Missouri (Missouri); Office of the Staff Judge Advocate (Fort Jackson). Retired, Colonel, 1983.

KRAWCIW, Nicholas S. H., Armor. Principal Assignments: 14th Armored Cavalry (Germany); Military Assistance Command (Vietnam); 1st Cavalry Division (Fort Hood); Tactical Department (West Point); 3d Squadron, 5th Cavalry (Vietnam); Naval War College (Rhode Island); Department of the Army (Pentagon); UN Truce Supervision Organization (Palestine); 1st Squadron, 2d Armored Cavalry (Germany); Headquarters, United States Army Europe (Germany); Army War College (Pennsylvania); Training and Doctrine Command (Fort Monroe); 3rd Armored Division (Germany); Supreme Headquarters, Allied Command Europe (Belgium); Department of the Army (Pentagon); 3d Infantry Division (Germany); NATO Policy, OSD (Pentagon). Retired, Major General, 1990.

McINERNEY, Thomas G., Infantry-USAF. Principal Assignments: 476th Tactical Fighter Squadron (George AFB); Military Assistance Command (Vietnam); 557th Tactical Fighter Squadron (Eglin AFB); Fighter Weapons School (Nellis AFB); 7th Air Force Liaison Officer (Vietnam); 469th Tactical Fighter Squadron (Thailand); Armed Forces Staff College (Virginia); Headquarters, USAF (Pentagon); National

War College (DC); George Washington University (DC); 58th Tactical Fighter Wing (Luke AFB); Air Attaché (United Kingdom); 20th Tactical Fighter Wing (United Kingdom); Office of the Secretary of Defense (Pentagon); 3d Tactical Fighter Wing (Philippines); 313th Air Division (Japan); Headquarters, Pacific Air Force (Hawaii); 3d Air Force (UK); United States Air Force-Europe (Germany); Alaska Command (Elmendorf AFB); Headquarters, USAF (Pentagon). Retired, Lieutenant General, 1994,

MULLEN, William J. III, Infantry. Principal Assignments: 3rd Infantry Division (Germany); Military Assistance Command (Vietnam); 2nd Infantry Division (Korea); 1st Battalion, 23rd Infantry (Ft. Benning); 1st Battalion, 2nd Infantry (Vietnam); Tactical Department (West Point); Naval Command & General Staff College (Rhode Island); George Washington University (DC); Department of the Army (Pentagon); 1st Infantry Division (Fort Riley); 1st Battalion, 2nd Infantry Regiment (Korea); I Corps (Korea); Army War College (Pennsylvania); 193rd Infantry Brigade (Panama); CENTCOM (Florida); 1st Brigade, 1st Infantry Division (Germany); 5th Infantry Division (Fort Polk); Combined Arms Test Activity (Fort Leavenworth); 1st Infantry Division (Germany & Kuwait); FORSCOM (Fort McPherson). Retired, Brigadier General, 1991.

O'MEARA, Andrew P., Jr., Armor. Principal Assignments: 1st Cavalry (Germany); V Corps Long Range Reconnaissance Patrol Company (Germany); Military Assistance Command (Vietnam); Armor School Training Command (Fort Knox); University of Wisconsin (Wisconsin); 11th Armored Cavalry (Vietnam); Command and General Staff College (Kansas); DISCOM, 4th Armored Division (Germany); 1st Battalion, 37th Armor (Germany); Headquarters, 4th Armored Division

(Germany); 2nd Brigade, 1st Armored Division (Germany); Foreign Area Specialist Training (Germany); 1st Battalion, 67th Armor (Fort Hood); Army War College (Pennsylvania); Department of the Army (Pentagon); Advanced Individual Training Brigade (Fort Knox); Army Training Board (Fort Eustis); 24th Infantry Division (Fort Stewart); National War College (DC). Retired, Colonel, 1989.

PHILLIPS, Alan B., Infantry. Principal Assignments: 51st Infantry (Germany); Military Assistance Command (Vietnam); 3d Training Regiment (Fort Dix); 173d Airborne Brigade (Vietnam); University of Massachusetts (Massachusetts); TIBd (Georgia); Command and General Staff College (Fort Leavenworth); 1st Battalion, 23rd Infantry (Korea); Department of the Army (Pentagon); 101st Airborne Division (Fort Campbell); Recruiting Command (New York); Industrial College of the Armed Forces (DC); NATO (Belgium); Defense Intelligence Agency (Pentagon); Defense Attaché (Belgium). Retired, Colonel, 1989.

REINHARD, Donald R., Artillery-Ordnance. Principal Assignments: 1st Battalion, 52d Air Defense Artillery (Camp Hanford); New Mexico State University (New Mexico); White Sands Missile Range (New Mexico); Department of Ordnance (West Point); 191st Ordnance Battalion, Ammo (Vietnam); Kansas Army Ammunition Plant (Parsons, Kansas); Command and General Staff College (Fort Leavenworth); U. S. Army, Ryukyu Islands (Okinawa); Army Materiel & Readiness Command (Virginia); Ballistic Research Laboratory (Aberdeen Proving Ground); Iowa Army Ammunition Plant (Middletown, Iowa); Standardization Group (United Kingdom); Ammunition Production Base Modernization Agency (Picatinny Arsenel); Armament, Munitions, and Chemical Command (Rock Island Arsenal). Retired, Colonel, 1987.

SCHWARTZ, William L., Infantry. Principal Assignments: 101st Airborne Division (Fort Campbell); Military Assistance Command (Vietnam); Infantry School (Fort Benning); American University (DC); Department of Social Sciences (West Point); 1st Cavalry Division (Vietnam); Sixth Army (California); Command and General Staff College (Fort Leavenworth); European Command (Germany); 91st (Training) Division (California). Retired, Lieutenant Colonel, 1980.

GLOSSARY

ADC	Assistant Division Commander
AF	Air Force
AFB	Air Force Base
AMMO	Ammunition
AO	Area of Operations
Article 15	Non-judicial punishment
C&C	Command and Control
CG	Commanding General
CINC	Commander in Chief
CO	Commanding Officer
CONUS	Continental United States
CP	Command Post
CSM	Command Sergeant Major
CW4	Chief Warrant Officer, W-4
Deadline	Inoperable Equipment

DOD	Department of Defense
DMZ	Demilitarized Zone
EPW	Enemy Prisoner of War
EUCOM	European Command
FORSCOM	Forces Command
HHC	Headquarters and Headquarters Company
IG	Inspector General
LFE	Large Force Exercise
LTC	Lieutenant Colonel
LZ	Landing Zone
M113	Armored, tracked personnel carrier
MOOTW	Military Operations Other than War
MOS	Military Occupation Specialty
MP	Military Policeman
NCO	Non-commissioned Officer
NLF	National Liberation Front
NVA	North Vietnamese Army
OP	Observation Post
PAVN	People's Army of (North) Vietnam
OJT	On-the-job training
OPTEMPO	Operations Tempo

PFC	Private First Class
RAF	Royal Air Force
R&R	Rest and Relaxation
RC	U.S. Army, Reserve Component
Ret	Retired
RPG	Rocket-propelled Grenade
S-2	Intelligence Officer
S-3	Operations Officer
S-4	Supply Officer
TFW	Tactical Fighter Wing
UCMJ	Uniform Code of Military Justice
USA	U.S. Army
USAF	U.S. Air Force
USAFE	U.S. Air Force-Europe
USAREUR	U.S. Army-Europe
USMC	U.S. Marine Corps
VC	Viet Cong
XO	Executive Officer

ACKNOWLEDGMENTS

Once written, books do not magically convert themselves, error free, into a printed text placed between attractive covers.
Achieving that outcome requires the effort of talented and dedicated experts who work well with the manuscript's authors.

We were fortunate to have had the support of just such a team. Heidi Roedel took our ideas and greatly improved upon them to create Leadership's *beautiful cover. Our manuscript's editor, Hazel Jay, demonstrated her sharp eye for detail and splendid mastery of style as she picked out errors we missed and improved and clarified many of our sentences. To Victoria Creamer fell the task of placing the book's photographs within the text and formatting it ready for printing. Aside from the skills they exercised on behalf of our book, each of them had a personality and manner that made preparing our manuscript for printing a most pleasant task even as we worked under the pressure of a looming deadline. They made the book happen.*

Nor should we forget our wives, who supported our efforts at every step of this yearlong project and tolerated seemingly endless monologues concerning the progress of our efforts. We owe them more than they may imagine.